Prudence
And Your Health

Mildred A. Martin

This workbook has been planned to accompany the book, *Prudence and the Millers*. Read the story chapter before doing each lesson.

This Book Belongs To

We have tried to ensure that the medical and anatomical information presented in this book is correct. Special thanks to Dr. Mark Kniss, M.D., reviewer.

The pictures in this book are primarily from Zedcor, Inc. and are used by permission. Other art includes original artwork by Esther King Fisher

Green Pastures Press

HC 67, Box 91-A • Mifflin, PA 17058
Printed in USA
ISBN 1-884377-07-6

Lesson 1
The Healthy Body

God has given each one of us a wonderful body.

Your healthy body has many things! It has a brain like a powerful computer, with a vast memory bank. It has a double-barreled pump which circulates 5,000 to 6,000 quarts of blood per day. It has thousands of miles of blood vessels, hundreds of muscles, thousands of hairs, and bones that are strong enough to carry thousands of pounds per square inch.

God spent a very short time creating the first human body; less than one day. But what a marvelous, complicated design He made in that short time! Doctors and scientists are still learning new things about our wonderful bodies. Medical doctors must study for many years before they can begin their work, but they still do not know nearly everything about the human body.

In this book we will study some of the parts and systems of your body. We will study some of the ways a prudent person can keep his body healthy. But we can never learn it all, because God is so infinitely great!

Look at the skin on the back of your hand. Do you think you "know it like the back of your hand"? A patch one inch square, which is only about one-twentieth of an inch thick, contains all these things:

9 feet of blood vessels
9,000 nerve endings
13 yards of nerves
300 sweat glands
600 pain sensors
36 heat sensors
6 cold sensors
4 oil glands
30 hairs

Prudence

The Bible tells us that we were created for God's glory and pleasure. If we are prudent, we will take good care of the bodies he has given us. Look at the pictures below and match each one with a rule for good health from the list below.

1. Prudent people keep themselves safe by following the laws of the land.

2. Prudent people do not eat too much, especially of sweets and "junk food."

3. People who follow God's laws will not fight and hurt or kill one another.

4. Prudence means being careful and cautious when we use tools that could be dangerous to our bodies.

5. Christians will keep their bodies clean and neat, for the glory of God.

6. "Wine is a mocker, strong drink is raging; whosoever is deceived thereby is not wise."

7. Prudent people eat good, fresh food that helps them to grow strong and healthy.

8. If we are prudent we will try to get enough sleep, so that our bodies can be at their best.

9. Prudent people wear clothes that are modest and protect their bodies from the weather.

10. Poisoning our bodies with tobacco smoke is not prudent!

Concordance Skill

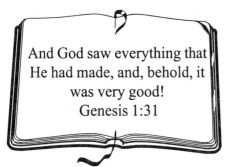

And God saw everything that He had made, and, behold, it was very good!
Genesis 1:31

In today's story, the Miller children used *concordances* to find the Scripture verses they wanted. Do you know how to use a *concordance*? Many Bibles have a simple concordance in their back pages. Maybe your bookshelf at home or at school also has a large book called a *Complete Concordance*. Using a concordance, find these Bible verses and copy them.

1. Which Bible verse, in the Psalms, describes how wonderfully God has created our bodies? (Concordance clue: look for the word *Fearfully*)

_____

_____

_____

2. Find a verse which tells us that God created us in his *image*:

_____

_____

_____

3. Which verse tells us what man is made of? (Concordance clue: use the word *dust*)

_____

_____

_____

4. Copy the verse that gives us the reason God created us. (Concordance clue: look for the word *pleasure*!)

_____

_____

_____

5. Find the two verses that tell who owns our bodies. (Clue: look up the word *temple*!)

_____

_____

_____

_____

_____

LESSON 2
Being Sick

Do you understand?

Find words in your story about *Timmy and the Lion*, to fill in te blanks below.

1. Colds are caused by tiny _____, called _____.

2. You catch the germs from somebody else who_____.

3. _____ can multiply inside your _____ and _____.

4. _____ are the protectors God gave our body, to
_____.

5. Why should you blow your nose gently when you have a cold? _____
_____.

6. Give two reasons why you should drink a lot when you are sick:_____
_____
_____.

7. What are some other things you can do to help yourself feel better? _____
_____
_____.

8. "Cover your _____ when you _____ ___ _____
Or your _____ will spread _____!"

9. Why should we stay home when we are sick? _____
_____.

More questions for you to think about!

1. What do you think would happen if a person who has a cold leaves his used tissues lying around for other people to handle? _____
_____.

2. Why do you think it is important for people to wash their hands before they eat? _____
_____.

3. What do you think will happen if a person who has a cold touches her friend's hands, and that friend rubs her eyes, or puts her fingers into her mouth?
_____.

Pills For All Ills?

In your story, Timmy took pills because of his high fever. Aspirin or Acetaminophen are common drugs that people take to reduce fever or relieve pain. All drugs and pills should be used with caution, though! Often there are better ways to deal with health problems than by taking pills.

Read each of the little stories below, and choose the *wisest* way for each member of the Brown family to handle his or her problem. Discuss your answers with your teacher or parents.

1. Mr. Brown has been working at his office desk all afternoon. Now he feels tired and tense, and his head is beginning to ache. Mr. Brown should:
> Drink a can of beer to help himself relax
> Take two aspirin pills
> Go outdoors for a brisk walk in the fresh air

2. Susie Brown has a hoarse, scratchy feeling in her throat. Susie could:
> Ask her mother to buy a bag of cherry-candy cough drops to keep in her desk.
> Take drinks of water often through the day, to keep her throat from drying out.

3. Mary Brown is overweight. "I'm tired of being so fat! It's time to do something about it," Mary says. Mary could:
> Start eating more fruit and vegetables instead of rich desserts, and get more exercise every day.
> Order some "Magic Weight Loss" pill that she saw in a magazine

4. Mrs. Brown often feels tired during the day. She should:
> Drink lots of coffee
> Buy some expensive pills from the health food store to give herself more "pep"
> Try to go to bed earlier at night

5. Little Matthew Brown fell down and cut his head. Now his skin looks red and swollen around the cut. Matthew's doctor says the cut is infected, and he must take antibiotic pills to kill the germs. Matthew should:
> Take the pills his doctor prescribed
> Wait awhile and see if the infection goes away by itself

Germ Hunters

People who lived long ago did not know anything about germs and viruses. They did not know what caused sickness, or how diseases spread from one person to another. Here are the names of four important men who made discoveries that would save many lives!

Look in your encyclopedia for each of these names, and find out which name answers each of the four riddles below.

Edward Jenner	Louis Pasteur
Anton van Leeuwenhoek	Joseph Lister

I was a Dutch cloth merchant who learned how to make glass lenses which could magnify tiny objects. In 1676 I discovered that I could see tiny living creatures in drops of water or in a person's saliva. I called these creatures "tiny animals," and drew pictures of the "tiny animals" which I saw under my microscope lens. I was the first person to see germs! Who am I?

_____

I was a French scientist who studied germs. I learned that germs multiply quickly in foods and drinks, causing them to spoil. I experimented with heating foods and drinks just enough to kill the germs. People today still use my method of heating milk to kill bacteria and keep it safe to drink. This method is called "pasteurization."

I also discovered how to vaccinate people who had been bitten by dogs with rabies, so that they would not die of the disease. Who am I?

_____

I was a doctor in Scotland who proved that germs caused infections in wounds. I taught other doctors to wash their hands before doing operations, and to sterilize the instruments they used. Besides teaching about the importance of cleanliness, I discovered how to use antiseptic solutions to kill germs. One kind of antiseptic that people still use for killing germs today, is called "Listerine" after me. Who am I?

_____

I was an English scientist who discovered how to vaccinate people to keep them from getting a deadly disease called smallpox. I learned that if a doctor scraped some germs from a sore on the arm of a person who was sick with a mild disease called "cowpox", and scratched these germs into the skin of a healthy person, that person would be safe from smallpox. This was the beginning of the use of shots to make people immune to certain diseases. Who am I?

_____

Why Do I Sleep?
Lesson 3

Everyone needs sleep. Sleep is the time when our body has its best chance to rest and recover from the work it has done during the day. Sleep heals our body and brain, and lets them store up energy for work and play.

In your story, you read about what happened to Sharon when she missed too much sleep. Losing sleep can make a person less alert. It also leaves the muscles tired, so that they don't carry out messages from the brain the way they should. This causes a person to be clumsy, to drop things and bump into things.

Some parts of your body keep working during sleep. Your heart keeps beating, and your lungs keep breathing. During sleep, though, the heart and lungs do not need to work so fast. Parts of your brain are still busy with dreams as you sleep. You dream about things that you have seen or heard or thought about while you were awake. Most people dream several times each night. A dream may last only a few minutes, or a whole hour. Most of our dreams are forgotten by the time we wake, but sometimes we remember them! What is one dream you remember?

A newborn baby will usually sleep at least 20 hours out of each 24-hour day. Small children must take a nap in the daytime besides sleeping at night. How old were you when you stopped taking an afternoon nap? Grown-ups usually do not sleep more than 8 hours a night, but 8 hours is still one-third of every 24-hour day! If we spend one-third of our lives sleeping, isn't that a big waste of time? No, because that is the way God planned for us to do.

Boys and girls your age need 9 to 10 hours of sleep every night to feel at your best. Draw hands on the first clock to show the time you usually go to bed. On the second clock, show the time you usually get up in the morning. How many hours of sleep do you get?

Sleepytime Puzzle

Down

1. Sharon's flashlight needed to be _____
2. God gives his beloved _____ (Psa. 127:2)
3. Lack of sleep made Sharon's brain _____
4. Lack of sleep makes a person's muscles _____
5. Sharon had a bad habit of _____ in bed
6. Time to go to sleep

Across

7. Our brain does this while we sleep
8. Small children need an afternoon _____
9. _____ need 8 hours of sleep a night
10. The night time is _____
11. Lack of sleep made Sharon's eyes lose their _____
12. Your _____ work more slowly during sleep
13. _____ needs sleep

For a Good Night's Sleep

1. Don't take trouble along to bed! The Bible says, "Let not the sun go down upon your wrath." If you are upset or worried about anything, pray about it or talk it over with your parents.

2. Do something quiet just before bedtime. Having family worship or listening to a bedtime story, or taking a nice warm bath are good ways to relax.

3. Try to go to bed about the same time each night.

4. Sleep in a dark, quiet room.

5. Your bedroom should be open to the fresh air in warm weather, and not overheated in cold weather.

6. Wear clean, comfortable night clothes for sleeping.

7. Your bed is for sleeping! When it is bedtime, do not read or play in bed.

GOOD NIGHT . . . SWEET DREAMS!

A Healthy Mind
Lesson 4

Your mind is part of the body God gave you. Your mind, or brain, controls your actions. What you do or don't do is decided by your mind. A healthy mind is a happy mind! We need to train our minds and attitudes to be healthy ones.

Strong feelings of anger, fear, or worry can cause changes in the way your body works. When you are afraid, your heartbeat and breathing speed up. When you are angry or upset, you will have trouble sleeping and digesting the food you eat. Worry may cause you to sweat and to have a "funny feeling" in your stomach.

If we have a habit of pitying ourselves, feeling pouty, grouchy, or rebellious, these wrong thoughts are like a poison in our minds. The Bible tells us that "As he thinketh in his heart, so is he." Proverbs 23:7

We will have healthier minds, *and* bodies, if we are in the habit of keeping our consciences clear and our attitudes cheerful.

Look up Proverbs 17:22, and fill in the missing words:

"A _____ _____ doeth _____ like a _____ : but a _____ _____ drieth the _____."

Turn to Philippians 4:8, and copy the list of six kinds of things that are good to think about! _____ _____ _____

_____ _____ _____

Your Skeleton

The Bible says that a guilty conscience affects even our bones! Here is a picture of your skeleton, or system of bones. Your bones are alive and growing. A baby's bones are soft, like the rubbery tip of your nose. As you grow older, the bones become coated with calcium phosphate, which comes mostly from milk. Gradually they turn hard. In an adult, though, about half of the bone mass is still made of living cells, blood vessels, and water. Your skull is the strong helmet of bone which protects your eyes and brain. It is made up of 29 bones together! Your heart and lungs are protected by a cage of ribs; most people have 24. Your back bone consists of 26 vertebrae. Your chest is also protected by the collarbone and the breastbone, or sternum. Your thighbone, called the femur, is the longest bone in your body. Your pelvis is the broad hip bone, and your shins have two bones each: the thicker tibia and the narrow fibula.

Our joints are a marvel of creation! With our elbows, wrists, knees and ankles we can bend, twist, stretch and swivel, point and pivot.

An adult skeleton consists of about 206 different bones! Can you label the basic parts on this picture?

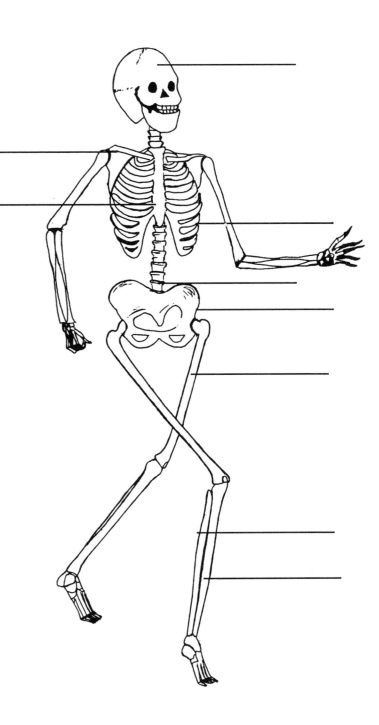

Healthy Attitudes

Read each story, and decide whether the child in the story shows a healthy attitude. Shade in the "Happy face" or the "Sad face" with your pencil or crayon!

1. Sarah thinks that the other children in her class don't want to play with her. At recess time she stays in her desk until all the others have gone outside, before walking slowly to the playground. When she comes out, she does not join in the game until the teacher says she must. ☺ ☹

2. Janie is a cheerful helper at home! She doesn't mind working, because she knows that things go more smoothly if everybody helps. She often asks her mother what she may do to help. Janie likes to sing as she works. ☺ ☹

3. Jim always blames other people when things happen to him. If he breaks something, or gets into trouble, he says that it was somebody else's fault. Jim's teacher told him that he has a bad attitude, but Jim thinks the teacher is picking on him. ☺ ☹

4. Two years ago Benjy stole a candy bar from the grocery store. Whenever he thinks about that candy bar now, Benjy feels embarrassed and guilty! But Benjy doesn't want to tell anybody what he did, so he tries to think about other things instead. ☺ ☹

5. Ruth Ann has many fears. She is afraid of dogs, afraid of the dark, and afraid of storms. She is afraid to try new foods, and she cries when she must go to the dentist. ☺ ☹

6. Ralph's parents and teachers are always glad when Ralph comes in! Ralph has such a bright smile, and he always says "Good Morning!" He is eager to try new lessons and games. ☺ ☹

7. Bonnie has a neighbor who is very unhappy. When this neighbor comes to visit Bonnie's parents, he grumbles and gossips about lots of different people. Bonnie likes to go to another room when the grouchy neighbor comes. "I don't want to listen to all those bad things about people!" Bonnie thinks. "I don't want to become cross and grouchy." ☺ ☹

Keeping Clean
Lesson 5

Our bodies are God's temple, and we should keep them clean! God created our bodies with a protective covering of skin. Our skin has two layers: the top layer is the *epidermis*, and the inside layer is called the *dermis*.

Our skin helps regulate our body heat, keeps germs and dirt out of the body, and helps to body get rid of wastes which could poison us and make us sick. As these wastes leave our body in our sweat, they collect on the skin and can cause an unpleasant smell if they are not washed away. When we are not clean, we are discourteous to others, and do not bring honor and glory to God!

On page 36 in your storybook, find the list of different times when the Book of Leviticus told people to bathe and wash their hands, and fill in the blanks below:

"God's people were to take _____ and _____ _____ _____ before they came to _____, after they _____ _____ _____ and after they had been with anyone else who was _____. The Jews washed their _____ before they _____, and bathed themselves whenever they happened to touch any _____ _____."

Here are some other times when you should wash your hands with soap and water:

Before you set the table or help with preparing food
After you play outdoors
After you work or play with animals
After you come home from town or other public places
After you use the bathroom

Can you think of more times when it is a good idea to wash your hands?

_____

_____

_____

Help Timmy Keep Clean

Here are eight hidden rules for healthy cleanliness. Unscramble the words and phrases and write them on the proper lines by this picture of Timmy.

-SHRUB ROUY HEETT
-LEACN OURY SAER
-WSHA ROUY OSHES
-MOCB RAHI
-RAEW LEACN LOCSETH
-NECLA SINGFERNIAL
-SHAW NADSH TEFON
-KEAT A THAB

Good Clean Fun

Find and circle these words in the puzzle below. How many of them have *you* used today?

bathtub	soap	towel	sink
toothbrush	water	comb	clean
washcloth	toothpaste	scrub	
bubbles	hairbrush	rinse	
shower	mirror	shampoo	

A	T	B	C	D	C	L	E	A	N	E
T	T	O	W	E	L	R	E	T	A	W
O	S	H	O	W	E	R	F	G	H	A
O	O	A	I	T	J	K	L	M	N	S
T	A	I	O	P	H	Q	R	S	T	H
H	P	R	B	U	B	B	L	E	S	C
P	S	B	U	M	I	R	R	O	R	L
A	I	R	B	A	T	H	T	U	B	O
S	N	U	V	W	B	U	R	C	S	T
T	K	S	X	R	I	N	S	E	Y	H
E	S	H	A	M	P	O	O	Z	A	B
A	G	R	N	C	O	M	B	O	I	L

Laura's Brushes
Lesson 6

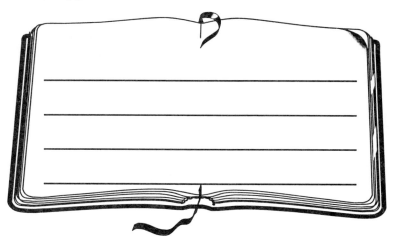

In your story today, Laura Miller counted five kinds of brushes which her family used to help keep clean and neat. Can you list them here?

_____

_____

_____

_____

_____

Mama told Laura that Christian people need to be clean and neat, or we will not bring honor and glory to God. Can you explain what she meant?

_____

_____

_____

_____

Copy I Corinthians 10:31 in the Bible below.

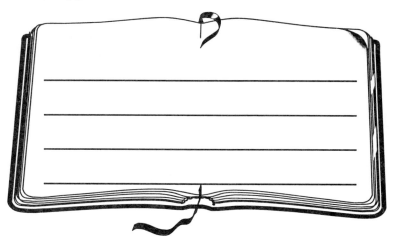

Your Teeth

What is the hardest thing in your body? Most people might answer "bones". But that's not the right answer! Your teeth are the hardest.

The outer layer of your teeth is called *enamel*. The enamel is almost totally made of minerals, and is like a rock. *Dentin* is the next layer. It is similar to bone, but harder. The inner part of your teeth is called *pulp*. This living center contains nerves and blood vessels. Each of your teeth is firmly rooted in its own spot in the jawbone.

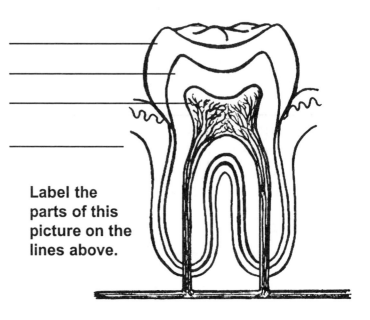

Label the parts of this picture on the lines above.

Why do you have so many different kinds and shapes of teeth in one mouth? God designed our mouths to be able to bite and chew a variety of different foods. In the front, we have 8 big flat teeth called *incisors*. These teeth work very much like scissors. They are your cutting teeth, for chopping out neat bites of food. Remember when you had several of your front teeth missing at the same time? It was probably very difficult for you to nip out bites of hard foods like apples or carrots!

Next in line are the sharp, pointy teeth called *canines*, which means "dog teeth". When you chew meat from a bone, you can see how these teeth got their name. There are four canines in your mouth, one in each corner.

Besides the canines are the *bicuspids*, meaning "two points". In the back of your mouth, last of all, are the *molars*. Molars are grindstones, to finish the job of chewing up your food.

Tooth enamel is hard stuff, but it can be damaged! Once your enamel is chipped or eaten away by acid, it can't repair itself. Many kinds of bacteria live in your mouth, and they eat the same food you do: bits of bread, potatoes, candy, and everything else. As they break down the food, these germs give off acid. It is very harmful for teeth to be covered by acid-making bacteria eating *their* lunch! This is why it is so important to brush your teeth after eating. Acid will eat holes, called *cavities*, in your tooth enamel.

Have you ever missed brushing your teeth for a long time? Soon your teeth began to feel as though fuzz is growing on them! That fuzzy stuff is called *plaque.* If plaque is left on your teeth, it hardens into yellow, crusty *tartar.* Tartar is very hard to clean off once it has hardened!

Caring For Your Teeth

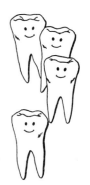

Leaving bits of food in your mouth is very bad for your teeth. Some foods are worse than others: sticky, gooey sweets, starchy foods, and acid drinks with a mixture of sweet and sour are the very worst. Some foods, though, are good tooth cleaners! And foods such as milk and cheese, which contain calcium, are also good for your teeth. In the box below are some different foods and drinks. Circle the ones which you think would be good for teeth, and cross out the ones which might be harmful.

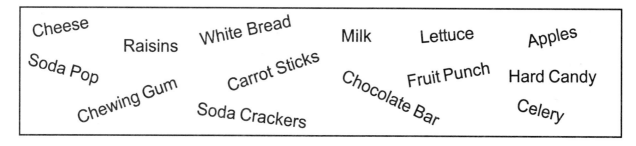

Cheese   Raisins   White Bread   Milk   Lettuce   Apples
Soda Pop   Carrot Sticks   Chocolate Bar   Fruit Punch   Hard Candy
Chewing Gum   Soda Crackers   Celery

Good Habits for Tooth Care

 Drink plenty of milk every day.

 Avoid sweets and sugary drinks.

 Do not try to crack nuts or chew ice with your teeth!

 Brush your teeth regularly, and use dental floss to clean between your teeth.

Go to the dentist for checkups, and to have tartar cleaned from your teeth.

Use toothpaste, mouthwash, or vitamins that have *fluoride* in them, to help protect your teeth.

Some interesting experiments to try:

1. Take one of your old teeth that has fallen out. Wrap it in a piece of cloth and tap it gently with a hammer until it splits apart. Can you see the different parts inside?

2. Open a small bottle of soda pop. Drop a tooth into the pop and close the cap of the bottle. Write the date on the bottle, and leave your tooth inside for a month or more. You can check the tooth every week, and see what is happening!

3. Buy some *disclosing tablets* at the drugstore, or ask your dentist for some. Follow the directions, and find out whether you are doing a good job of brushing *your* teeth!

Hot-Shot Henry
Lesson 7

Following the rules will keep us safe from a lot of pain and grief! Wise boys and girls will understand that older people have more experience than they do, and make rules for their own good. Read the stories below. Write <u>HH</u> for "Hotshot Henry," or <u>PP</u> for "Prudent Peter" in the blanks after each one.

1. In the town where Richard lives, it is the law that bicycle riders must wear helmets. "That's a stupid law!" says Richard. He never wears a helmet, and is always looking nervously over his shoulder to see if any police officers are in sight. _____

2. Rosa makes sure that her bike tires are firmly inflated, and the nuts that hold her wheels in place are tight, before she goes for a ride. _____

3. Marcus is teaching his little sister how to ride a bike. He shows her how to make the hand signals for "right turn", "left turn", and "stop". They practice the signals many times as they ride back and forth in the lane. _____

4. Paul likes to carry his friend Andrew on the handlebars of his bike as they go down the road. "You can tell me which way to go!" Paul laughs. _____

5. Lauren always rides her bike in the same direction that the cars are going on the highway. _____

6. "Those rules are for the little tots," Timothy snickered. "I'm eleven years old. What does it matter if I ride with no hands, or do any tricks I feel like doing?" _____

7. "Let's beat that train!" Chris whooped as he and Jason raced their bikes toward the railroad tracks. The gates were coming down, but both boys were sure they could make it through. _____

8. Sarah uses a dry rag to wipe her bicycle clean after she rides in the rain or slush, so that it will not get rusty. _____

9. Martha's brakes don't always work, but she figures that she can stop her bicycle by dragging her feet in the gravel. _____

10. "I'll race you to the bottom of the hill!" cried Tom. "Bet we will be doing forty-five miles an hour by the time we get there!" _____

20

Exercise

Riding bicycle is good exercise. Our bodies need exercise every day in order to be healthy. When a person gets enough exercise to be in good condition, we say that they are "physically fit". All their muscles, including the important heart muscle, are strong and firm. A person who is physically fit can work and play without getting tired too soon. He can feel better, sleep better, and eat better than a person who does not get proper exercise.

Exercise helps us grow. It makes our muscles strong, and our balance better. Boys and girls who are physically fit will look healthier and more attractive, too, than those who sit around and watch television!

Hard work is good for our bodies, and so are active games. Look at the list of activities below, and decide which group they belong to. Copy each activity under one of the three headings. The first ones are done for you.

Vigorous Exercise

digging in the garden

_____

_____

_____

_____

Mild Exercise

walking

_____

_____

_____

_____

Little or No Exercise

sitting in the yard

_____

_____

_____

Reading
Running up the stairs
Sitting in church
Riding a bicycle fast
Jogging
Sewing
Picking berries
Climbing a tree
Playing softball
Sweeping
Hanging up wash
Playing checkers
Digging in the garden
Walking
Sitting in the yard

Do you get some *vigorous exercise* every day?

Your Muscles

You could not do any exercise if you had no muscles! The human body has more than 600 different muscles. If all your muscles were used to pull together in one direction they could pull with a force equal to 25 tons. Muscle mass makes up about one-half of your body.

You have 3 different kinds of muscles. *Skeletal* muscles are the ones that move your bones around. Skeletal muscles move when they get messages from your brain. They let you use your arms and legs, turn your head, or blink your eyes.

When you are running a race, riding your bike uphill, or carrying a heavy load, your muscles begin to burn with pain after awhile. You are forced to stop and take a rest. Why? Your muscles need to use oxygen when they work. Your heart pounds and you gasp for breath, trying to suck in oxygen for your muscles as fast as they can. Sometimes you can't do it fast enough, and your muscles refuse to work anymore until they "catch up" on oxygen.

Smooth muscles work automatically, doing things like keeping your throat clear and pumping food around in your stomach.

Cardiac muscle is the special, strong muscle which makes up your heart. If you hold a tennis ball in your hand and squeeze it hard seventy times every minute for several minutes, you will have some idea of the work your heart must do.

Your Eyes
Lesson 8

"The hearing ear, and the seeing eye, the Lord hath made even both of them!" Proverbs 20:12.

Your eye is a tough little bag a bit smaller than a ping-pong ball, full of a clear jelly-like fluid. At the front of the bag is a window that lets in light. This window is covered by the *cornea*, which acts like a camera lens.

The dark spot in the center of your eye is the *pupil*. Your pupil changes its size in response to light. The colored ring around your pupil is the *iris*. This colored iris uses a set of tiny muscles to open your pupil wider in the dark, or shrink it down more tightly when you are in a brightly lighted place.

Your *retina* changes light into nerve impulses, which are sent into your brain by the optic nerve. Your brain then tells you what you are seeing!

The *lens* in your eye helps you focus by becoming longer or shorter. Hold up one finger about ten inches in front of your face. Slowly bring your finger closer to your eyes, as you keep focusing on it. Do you feel the tiny muscles straining inside your eye? These are the muscles that do not work well enough in the eye of a *nearsighted* person, like Mama and Peter Miller in your story. Nearsighted people can see better with corrective lenses called eyeglasses.

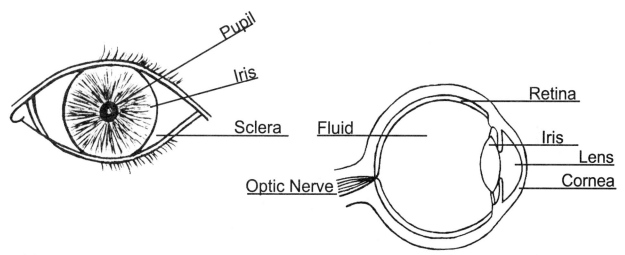

Your eyes are protected by the hard, bony skull, by your bushy eyebrows and eyelashes, and by the skin of your eyelid, which clamps down tightly if anything comes near your eye. Eyes are very delicate, and you must take care not to damage them.

Louis Braille was the son of a shoemaker in France in the early 1800's. When he was a little boy, he accidently damaged his eye with his father's sharp pointed tool called an awl. Louis' eyes became infected, and he grew totally blind. When Louis grew up, he invented Braille writing, a system of raised dots that blind people can "read" by feeling with their fingertips.

Do You Know?

Match these words with their meanings:

1. Nearsighted	A clear covering over the lens of your eye
2. Iris	The dark spot in the center of your eye
3. Cornea	The white part of your eye
4. Pupil	The colored part of the eye
5. Louis Braille	An eye problem which makes it hard to focus on things that are far away
6. Retina	Carries messages between eye and brain
7. Sclera	Light-sensitive area in the back of your eyeball
8. Optic Nerve	Invented a special alphabet for blind people

True or False

1. Your eyes can work best to read when you lie down _____
2. You should not look at the sun or other bright lights _____
3. Your book should be held about 18 inches away from your face _____
4. If you often have headaches, your eyes may need to be checked _____
5. Jesus was able to heal people who were blind _____
6. Children should try on other people's glasses to see how they work _____
7. A nearsighted person cannot see things that are near him _____
8. Your eyelids close automatically if anything comes near your eye _____
9. The pupils of your eyes shrink in response to bright light _____
10. Your eyeball is full of air like a balloon _____

Your Ears

How about your ears? The part of the ear that you can see is called the outer ear, or *auricle*. But all the really important parts of your ear are on to inside! That dark tunnel going into your ear is called the *ear canal*. At the end of this canal is the *eardrum*, a thin skin much like the cover of a drum. Sounds coming down the ear canal make this drum vibrate. These vibrations are passed on next to three little bones. First of all is the *hammer*, attached to the drum. This passes vibrations on to the *anvil*, and the anvil sends them to the *stirrup*. Sound waves from the stirrup pass in to the *cochlea*, a bony tube shaped like a snail and full of fluid. Vibrations in the fluid are picked up by tiny hairs which send nerve signals to the brain. At last your brain understands what you have heard: but this whole process of hearing happens in just an instant!

God has created our ears in a wonderful way, and He expects us to take good care of them. Keep your ears clean, and protect them from getting hit! Keep your ears warm when you are outdoors in the cold wind. Never poke anything into your ears, or anyone else's ears. Try to protect your ears from noise that is too loud. Listening to loud music, or machinery, can damage your ears permanently.

Try this! Number these words or phrases from one to ten, showing the correct order in which they happen. The first one is done for you.

__1.__ The telephone rings

_____ cochlea

_____ eardrum vibrates

_____ auricle or outer ear catches the sound

_____ stirrup

_____ anvil

_____ hammer

_____ nerve signals

_____ you answer, "Hello!"

Fire Safety
Lesson 9

Playing with fire may be a thrill, but fires can kill! Timmy and his friends in your story experienced just a little of the power of fire. Any boy or girl who has ever seen a house or barn that burned down, or met a real person who was burned and scarred by fire, or known of people who died when their house burned, will have great respect for that danger!

Read Timmy Miller's Fire Safety Rules again, and fill in the blanks below.

1. Never play with _____, _____, _____, or other things used for _____ _____.

2. If you see _____ _____ _____ _____ _____, tell an adult immediately.

3. Keep _____ or _____ away from _____ and _____.

4. Keep _____, _____, _____, _____ or _____ _____ away from heat.

5. Never _____ _____.

6. Do not use _____ _____ with _____ or _____ _____.

7. If your _____ ever _____ _____, do not _____. Stop, _____ _____ _____ _____ and _____ _____ to smother the flame.

8. Be sure your family has a _____ _____ _____ at home.

Behold, how _____ _____ _____ a little _____ _____. James 3:5

Review Time!

How much do you remember? Circle the right answer.

1. School-age children should sleep at least _____ hours every night.
   eight   nine   twelve

2. The man who first saw germs in a microscope was:
   Leuwenhoek   Lister   Jenner

3. Your back bones are called:
   tibias   vertebrae   sternums

4. An adult skeleton has about _____ bones. 155   190   206

5. The longest bone in your body is the: femur   fibula   fixus

6. The outer layer of your skin is called the:
   dermis   epidermis   endodermis

7. The muscles that move your body around are the _____ muscles.
   smooth   cardiac   skeletal

8. The colored part of your eye is called the:
   iris   pupil   retina

9. When you read, your page should be about _____ from your face.
   10 inches   18 inches   30 inches

10. The man who invented an alphabet for the blind was:
    Louis Braille   Louis Charbonneau   Joseph Lister

Match these words with their meanings.

11. pupil ___
12. lens ___
13. optic nerve ___
14. cardiac muscle ___
15. oxygen ___
16. plague ___
17. enamel ___
18. molars ___
19. ribs ___
20. aspirin ___

a. carries messages from eye to brain
b. your muscles need this when they work
c. part of your eye that changes its size in response to light
d. eye muscle that helps you focus
e. fuzzy stuff that forms on teeth
f. grinding teeth in the back of your mouth
g. most people have 24
h. pills which can be taken for fever
i. outer layer of your teeth
j. heart muscle

21. Name three kinds of attitudes that are unhealthy.

_____

_____

_____

22. List four times when it is important to wash your hands:

_____

_____

_____

_____

23. Why should Christian people always try to be clean and neat?

_____

_____

24. Find and copy a Bible verse that tells to whom our bodies belong.

_____

_____

25. Why should we stay home from school or church when we are sick?

_____

_____

26. Name three ways we can help get ready for a good night's sleep:

_____

_____

_____

27. List three good habits for taking care of your teeth:

_____

_____

_____

28. Name three ways that <u>you</u> got good exercise in the past week!

_____

_____

29. List two good rules for ear care and safety:

_____

_____

30. Name three things God gave us to protect our delicate eyes:

_____

_____

_____

Foods We Need
Lesson 10

When Sharon did the cooking, she planned healthy meals using these four basic groups of food. Study this table and see why your body needs the different groups.

Food Group	What's in it	What it does for you	Good choices
Vegetable and Fruit Group	Vitamin C Vitamin A Vitamin K Vitamin E Fiber Natural Sugar	Protects the body from sickness, and helps fight infection.. Gives you energy. Helps skin and eyes to be at their best. Helps the body eliminate wastes. Helps blood clot if skin is cut.	
Bread and Cereal Group	Carbohydrates Vitamin B Vitamin E Fiber	Supplies energy for work and play. Helps your body use other foods. Strengthens your heart.	
Milk Group	Calcium Phosphorous Vitamin D	Builds strong bones and teeth. Helps your muscles and nerves work the way they should.	
Meat, Beans, Nuts and Fish Group	Protein Iron Vitamin A & B Fats Iodine	Helps you grow. Repairs body tissues. Helps digestion. Makes red blood cells to carry oxygen through your body. Needed for good vision and smooth skin.	

Growing boys and girls your age need to eat some foods from each group every day. You should have at least 4 servings from the bread group and the fruit-vegetable group each day, 2 servings from the meat group, and 2 or 3 servings of milk, yogurt, or cheese.

You Do the Cooking!

If it were up to you to chose the menu for one day, as Sharon Miller did, what foods would you choose? Plan a day of three healthy meals for yourself, and list the foods you would eat. Remember to use 4 different fruits or vegetables, 4 servings of bread or other grain foods, two servings of meat, eggs or beans, and 3 servings from the milk group! Draw a picture of each meal.

Breakfast

Lunch

Supper or Dinner

The Fourth Meal

If you are like most boys and girls, you usually eat more than 3 meals a day! Usually you also eat some snacks between meals, like after school or before bedtime. A snack can be your fourth meal of the day, and you need to choose snack foods wisely. Candy, pop, and chips may taste good, but they do not have the nutrients your body needs to grow and be healthy! Look at the many different snack choices listed below. Circle the ones that would make a good healthy snack, and cross out the unwise choices.

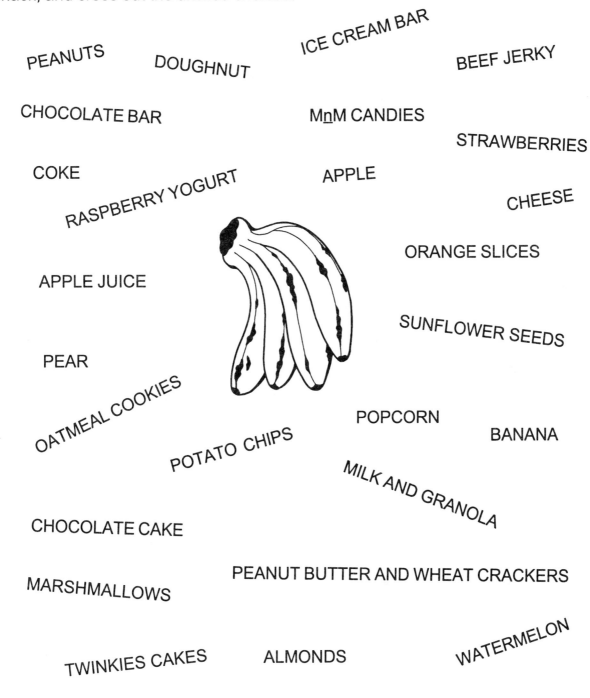

PEANUTS   DOUGHNUT   ICE CREAM BAR   BEEF JERKY

CHOCOLATE BAR   MnM CANDIES

STRAWBERRIES

COKE   APPLE   CHEESE

RASPBERRY YOGURT

ORANGE SLICES

APPLE JUICE

SUNFLOWER SEEDS

PEAR

OATMEAL COOKIES

POPCORN   BANANA

POTATO CHIPS

MILK AND GRANOLA

CHOCOLATE CAKE

PEANUT BUTTER AND WHEAT CRACKERS

MARSHMALLOWS

WATERMELON

TWINKIES CAKES   ALMONDS

31

Lesson 11
How You Breathe

Your vocal cords are the "voice box" that makes sound. Your lungs are about the size of a pair of footballs! They fill your chest from the neck to the bottom of your ribs.

All living things need oxygen to survive! God gave us lungs to pump in air and separate out the precious oxygen so our bodies can use it.

After air is sucked in through your mouth or nose, it goes down the windpipe and enters your lungs through the bronchial tubes. Your lungs have millions of spongy little bags called alveoli, which pull out the oxygen and send it through the lung walls.

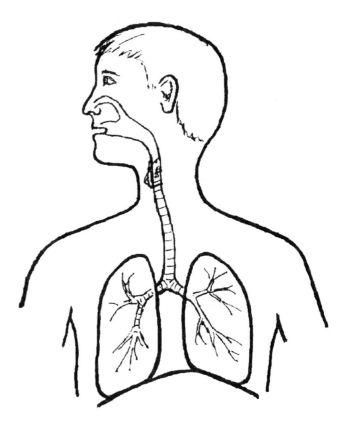

Your diaphragm muscle moves up and down, squeezing air in and out of your lungs.

How fast do you breathe? Your rate of breathing is controlled automatically by your brain. The respiratory center of your brain calls on your lungs to breathe just as fast as you need to breathe at each moment: Slow for sleeping, faster for running!

Running a 100-yard race takes about seven quarts of oxygen. There is usually about one quart of oxygen already in your blood, so your lungs will need to provide the rest!

Watch a clock, and count how many times you breathe during one minute while you are sitting quietly at your desk. Now spend a few minutes running or jumping up and down, then count your breaths per minute again. See the difference?

Hiccups, Burps, and other Funny Things

Your respiratory (breathing) system can do all kinds of tricks! Read the little stories below and decide which of the words in the box is the right name for what is happening.

> **sneeze   hiccups   cough**
> **smell   yawn   sing   burp**

1. You have smelled something that makes your nose prickle and tickle. A nerve reflex makes you gasp for air, then sends the air exploding out again through your nose and mouth, along with a spray of water droplets from your mouth. Cover your mouth! You are going to _____

2. You have a cold, and mucus is dripping down the back of your throat. God has designed your body with a safety reflex to keep things out of your windpipe, so that you will not choke. This reflex forces a powerful blast of air back up your throat to blow the mucus out and, you will _____

3. You were eating too fast, and some air got into your stomach along with the food. Your diaphragm muscle squeezes, and a puff of air comes back up and out your mouth. Say "excuse me!" when you _____

4. Your diaphragm muscle has started contracting in jerks, making air rush into your lungs. To stop it, a lid called the epiglottis claps down and closes the top of your windpipe. Your whole body is shaken by the sudden opening and shutting. You have _____

5. You are sitting in school listening to the teacher explain a boring math problem, and you have been feeling sleepy, so you have been breathing too shallowly. Suddenly your brain calls for a deeper breath, and your mouth is forced open to pull in air. This is called a _____

6. Air is passing through your vocal cords, making them vibrate, while the sound bounces into your mouth and nose passages. Stretching your vocal cords as tightly as you can makes a higher-pitched sound, and relaxing them produces low, deep sounds. This is how you _____

7. Dinner is cooking, and tiny invisible particles are floating through the air. Some of the tiny bits enter your nose, and tiny hairs called <u>olfactory rods</u> sends signals to the nerve cells in your brain. Your brain figures out what's cooking! This is how you _____

The Breath of Life

How much do you remember? Fill the blanks with the correct words.

1. "And the _____ _____ formed man of the _____ of the ground, and _____ into his _____ the _____ of _____; and man became a _____ _____." Genesis 2:7

2. Breathing properly gets more _____ to our body cells, so we can be _____ and not get _____ so easily.

3. Inside your lungs are _____ of tiny spongy air sacs called _____.

4. _____ _____ is a gas our body must get rid of.

5. You should never even try one _____!

6. Good _____ helps us to breathe properly, so that our _____ will not be crowded.

7. It is better to breathe through your _____, with the mouth _____. Your nose _____ and _____ the air.

8. Babies can choke on _____ that are popped.

9. Don't put _____ _____ over your head.

10. Never _____ anything around anyone's neck.

11. Never get into an empty _____ or _____, or any other _____ place.

12. Four little boy's faces turned _____ from lack of oxygen!

13. Without the breath of life, we will _____.

14. Your _____ _____ are the voice box that produces sound.

15. Your lungs are about the size of _____.

16. _____ tubes are the gateways from windpipe to lungs.

17. The _____ center of your brain regulates your breathing system.

Water Safety
Lesson 12

Draw a line from the phrase in column A to the phrase in column B that finishes the rule about water safety.

A.	B.
1. Do not go swimming alone	to swim.
2. Learn how	when you are riding in a boat.
3. Wear a life jacket	you have eaten a big meal.
4. Stay away from water	in case you have any trouble.
5. Do not swim right after	during a thunderstorm.
6. Don't push or tease	call for help in the water!
7. Never dive into water	you aren't sure about.
8. Never jokingly	common sense.
9. Do not stand up	your friends in the water.
10. Use	in a boat.

Find the Hidden Message

Take a dark blue pencil or crayon and color each block that has the letters C, O, X or T. The letters that are left will spell a secret message. Copy it on the line below.

C	T	S	O	W	X	I	M	C	O	X	T
S	X	E	N	C	S	I	O	B	L	Y	C
T	S	C	W	O	I	X	M	T	C	O	X
X	O	S	A	C	F	O	E	L	Y	T	O

Your Heart

"Keep thy heart with all diligence; for out of it are the issues of life." Proverbs 4:23. Your heart is a very vital, necessary organ of your body. You could do without a leg, an eye, or an ear; but if your heart stops, you will die!

Your heart is actually *two* pumps working as a team. The pump on the right brings "tired" blood into your lungs, where it picks up oxygen. The one on the left pumps fresh blood, full of oxygen, through the arteries of your body. In . . . out, in . . . out! This is what King Solomon meant about the "issues of life!"

Your heart is about the same size as your fist. Your body contains between three and six quarts of blood, depending on the size of your body. The heart circulates all your blood back and forth more than 1000 times per day, pumping it along many thousands of miles of blood vessels! If all the blood vessels in your body were laid out in a straight line, there would be about 60,000 miles of them.

You have three different kinds of blood vessels in your body. The *arteries* carry fresh blood from your heart. They are tough tubes that can stand the fast rush of blood pulsing under pressure!

Your *veins* carry the "tired" blood back into your heart and lungs. The blood moves more slowly through your veins. Veins are the blood vessels that look like blue lines under your skin.

Capillaries are the tiny blood vessels, smaller than a hair. These thin, delicate blood vessels nourish every cell in your body. If you would like to get a good look at all three kinds of blood vessels, take a mirror and stand under a good light. Now look at the underside of your tongue! Can you see the thick pink artery? The blue veins? The tiny, hairlike capillaries?

Take the empty tube from a roll of paper towels, and use it like a stethoscope. Listen to a young child's heart beat. Now listen to a grown-up's heartbeat. Which beats faster?

Heart Puzzle

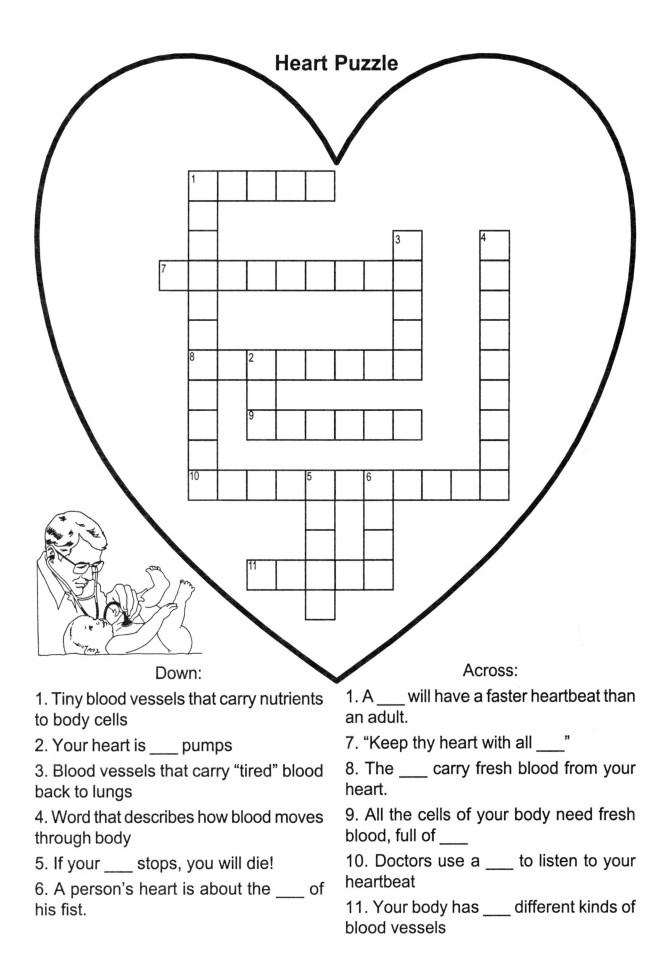

Down:

1. Tiny blood vessels that carry nutrients to body cells

2. Your heart is ___ pumps

3. Blood vessels that carry "tired" blood back to lungs

4. Word that describes how blood moves through body

5. If your ___ stops, you will die!

6. A person's heart is about the ___ of his fist.

Across:

1. A ___ will have a faster heartbeat than an adult.

7. "Keep thy heart with all ___"

8. The ___ carry fresh blood from your heart.

9. All the cells of your body need fresh blood, full of ___

10. Doctors use a ___ to listen to your heartbeat

11. Your body has ___ different kinds of blood vessels

Your Digestion
Lesson 13

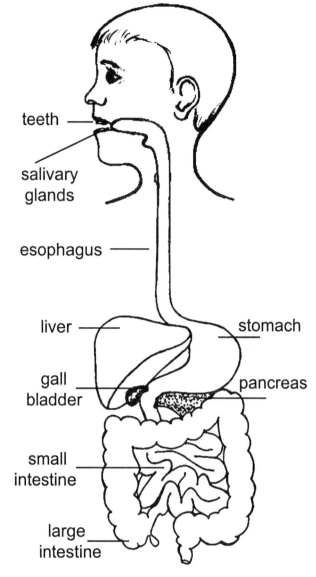

teeth

salivary glands

esophagus

liver

gall bladder

stomach

pancreas

small intestine

large intestine

What happens when you take a bite of food? First of all, your teeth and tongue chop and grind the food into bits. Liquid called *saliva* comes from the *salivary glands*. You can feel a salivary gland in your mouth if you touch your tongue to the area above your back teeth. Feel that little bump under the skin?

When a bite of food has been chewed enough, your tongue pushes it to the back of your mouth, and you swallow. Strong muscles squeeze the food down the long tube called the *esophagus*, so that you could swallow even if you were upside down!

In the stomach, your food is sqeezed and churned around, and mixed with other digestive enzymes and acids. These "digestive juices" turn the food into liquid, which is gradually squeezed from the stomach into your small intestine. Your stomach can hold one and a half quarts at a time, but we usually do not eat that much at a meal. In 3 or 4 hours after eating a meal, that food has left your stomach, and you feel "hungry" again for another meal.

Your liver, gall bladder, and pancreas all make digestive juices and acids to help your body use the food you eat. These juices mix with the food in your *small intestine,* a curly tube about 20 feet long. Now the food is completely digested, and it is absorbed through the walls of the small intestine into your bloodstream by tiny tubes called *villi*. Your small intestine is a noisy place, as the muscles squeeze, squash, and squirt your food around! To hear the activity going on inside the intestines, try this: have a friend lie on his back. Press your ear gently against your friend's belly. What do you hear?

The large intestine is shorter than the "small" one, but it is much thicker. This big tube collects all the things that could not be digested, like celery strings and blackberry seeds and the gum you swallowed by accident. This waste material piles up in the large intestine, together with some dead bacteria, until it gets pushed out into the toilet.

Temperance Means Self-Control!

In today's story, Timmy Miller learned about the dangers of being greedy. Temperance is one of the most important health rules! We must control ourselves, and not let our bodies' desires rule over us. Overdoing anything can be unhealthy. Read these scripture verses, and fill in the blanks:

Proverbs 25:16 Hast thou found _____? Eat so _____ as is _____ for thee, lest _____ be _____ _____, and _____ _____.

Romans 6:12 Let not _____ therefore _____ in your _____ _____, that ye should _____ it in the _____ _____.

Proverbs 23:21+22. Be _____ among _____; among _____ eaters of _____: For the _____ and the _____ shall come to _____, and _____ shall clothe a _____ with _____.

I Corinthians 9:25. And every _____ that _____ for the _____ is _____ in _____ _____.

Who was temperate, and who was greedy? Read the little stories below, and write the names of each child into the list where they belong.

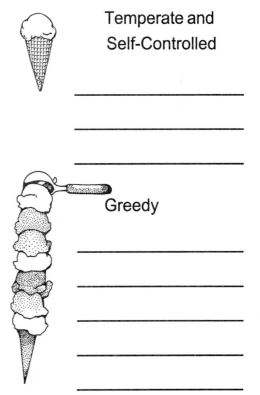

Temperate and
Self-Controlled

_____

_____

_____

Greedy

_____

_____

_____

_____

1. Judy and Joe went to a birthday party. Judy ate just one cupcake, taking small bites and enjoying each one, but Joe gobbled up four of them before he was satisfied.

2. When Sally and Sam's mother calls them in the morning, Sam gets up right away to help his mother with breakfast. Sally feels so cozy and drowsy! She just lies there and goes back to sleep until Mother calls again.

3. Larry and Lamar decide to have a contest: who can drink a 24 oz. bottle of Mountain Dew the fastest?

4. Marvin and Mary have new library books that are exciting to read! Marvin reads a few chapters, then puts the book away. He will save some for another day. Mary is determined to finish the whole book in one evening! She keeps on reading, even though her head hurts and her eyes burn.

Apples, Apples!

What happens to your apple when you eat a snack? Number these steps in digestion from one to nine. The first one is done for you.

Your front teeth cut out a bite of apple ①

Strong muscles squeeze it down the esophagus

The apple enters your small intestine

Your molars grind the apple to mush

Your stomach mixes the apple with acids

You swallow the bite

Vitamins from your apple go through the villi

Digestive juices from your liver and pancreas, mix with the apple

Your bloodstream carries the vitamins through your body

God has created so many different kinds of juicy, healthful fruits for us to enjoy! Can you find and circle twenty of them in the puzzle below?

A	A	P	R	I	C	O	T	B	C	D	E	R
O	B	A	N	A	N	A	P	L	U	M	S	G
R	F	L	G	H	I	R	R	A	J	K	L	R
A	M	N	U	P	O	P	W	C	Q	R	R	A
N	S	T	A	E	C	U	A	K	I	W	I	P
G	R	A	P	E	B	H	T	B	V	W	X	E
E	Y	P	E	A	R	E	E	E	Z	A	B	F
S	T	R	A	W	B	E	R	R	I	E	S	R
C	D	R	C	R	E	F	M	R	R	G	H	U
A	I	J	H	K	L	M	E	I	I	I	N	I
P	I	N	E	A	P	P	L	E	O	E	E	T
P	P	Q	S	R	R	S	O	S	T	U	S	S
L	E	M	O	N	M	A	N	G	O	V	W	X
E	Y	R	R	Y	G	U	A	V	A	Z	A	B

Safety at Home
Lesson 14

Do you know the safety rules? Fill in the blanks below to complete each sentence.

1. Never leave anything lying on a _____.

2. _____ children go to the doctor every _____ because of _____ which happened at _____.

3. Always drain the _____ when you are finished bathing, close the lid of the _____, and don't leave _____ standing around with water in them.

4. Cleaning supplies, medicines, gasoline, and kerosene can be _____.

5. Never put anything strange into your mouth until you ask your _____ if it is safe to eat.

6. When you are mowing grass, make sure there are no small _____ close by. Check the grass for objects that could be _____ by the mower blades.

7. When you carry a knife or scissors, hold it by the _____ with the sharp part pointing _____.

8. If you hand a sharp tool to someone else, hold it by the _____ and give the other person the _____.

9. Never throw a _____ or _____, and never _____ one from another person.

10. When you _____ with a knife, move the blade _____ from yourself.

11. When you are finished with a _____ _____, put it _____ at once!

12. Do not take _____ like candy.

13. "Hear, O my _____, and _____ my _____, and the years of thy _____ shall be _____. I have _____ thee in the _____ of _____; I have led _____ in _____ _____." Proverbs 4:10-12

14. _____ and _____ will help to keep us safe.

41

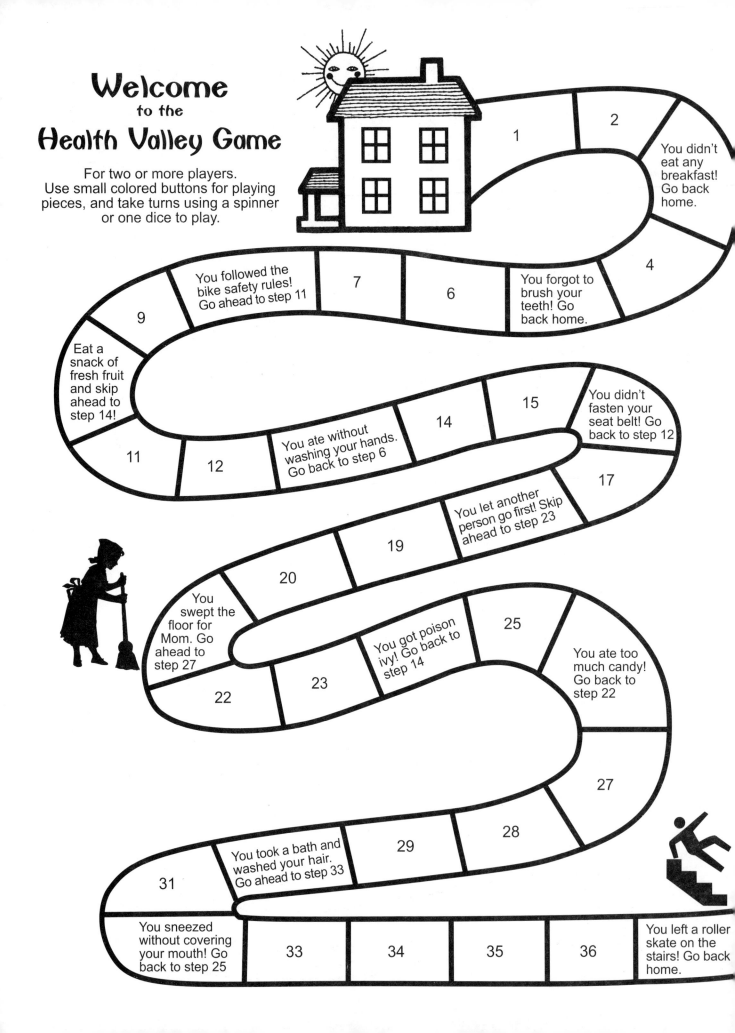

Welcome
to the
Health Valley Game

For two or more players.
Use small colored buttons for playing
pieces, and take turns using a spinner
or one dice to play.

1

2

You didn't eat any breakfast! Go back home.

4

You forgot to brush your teeth! Go back home.

6

7

You followed the bike safety rules! Go ahead to step 11

9

Eat a snack of fresh fruit and skip ahead to step 14!

11

12

You ate without washing your hands. Go back to step 6

14

15

You didn't fasten your seat belt! Go back to step 12

17

You let another person go first! Skip ahead to step 23

19

20

You swept the floor for Mom. Go ahead to step 27

22

23

You got poison ivy! Go back to step 14

25

You ate too much candy! Go back to step 22

27

28

29

You took a bath and washed your hair. Go ahead to step 33

31

You sneezed without covering your mouth! Go back to step 25

33

34

35

36

You left a roller skate on the stairs! Go back home.

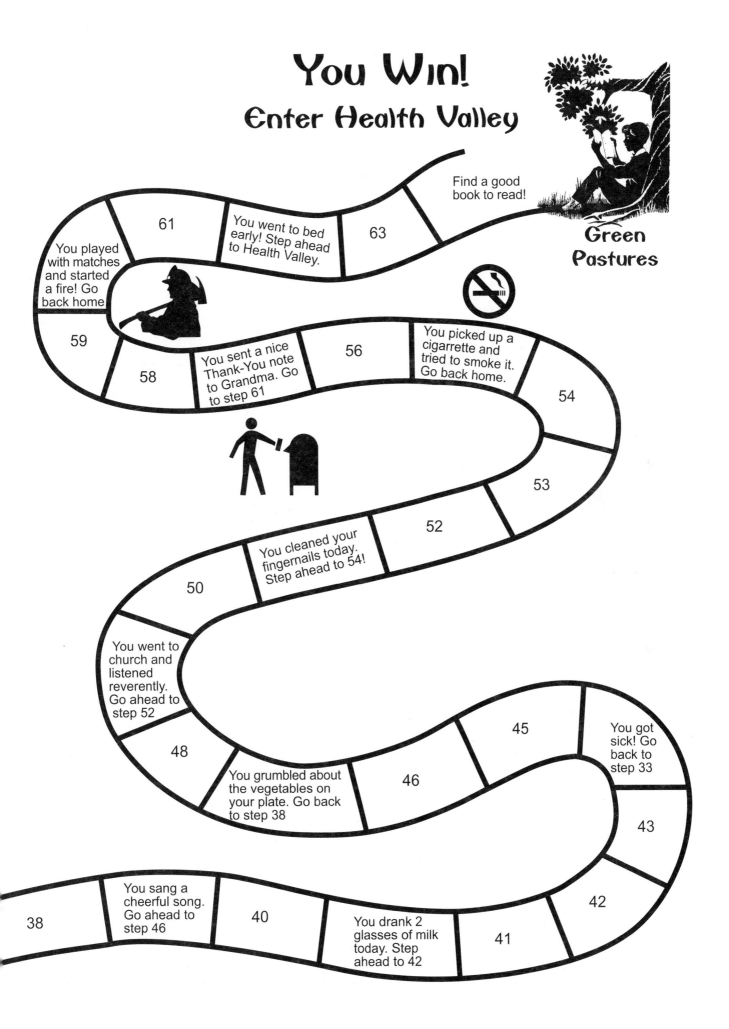

You Win!
Enter Health Valley

Find a good book to read!

Green Pastures

61

You went to bed early! Step ahead to Health Valley.

63

You played with matches and started a fire! Go back home

59

58

You sent a nice Thank-You note to Grandma. Go to step 61

56

You picked up a cigarrette and tried to smoke it. Go back home.

54

53

52

You cleaned your fingernails today. Step ahead to 54!

50

You went to church and listened reverently. Go ahead to step 52

48

You grumbled about the vegetables on your plate. Go back to step 38

46

45

You got sick! Go back to step 33

43

42

38

You sang a cheerful song. Go ahead to step 46

40

You drank 2 glasses of milk today. Step ahead to 42

41

A Dangerous Place

You may use this page to draw a picture of a room, or more than one room, of a house where people are not following good safety rules. Try to show at least five things that are dangerous in your picture. You may use ideas from your story today, and also from page 63 in your storybook.

You Decide!

Here are 8 short stories of accidents that have happened to real people. Read each one, and use the lines after it to tell how you think the accident could have been prevented.

1. Little Nathan was standing up in his highchair. He fell out and landed on his head, getting a bad cut that needed stitches. _____
_____

2. Rosina's cousin was burning trash. He poured gasoline on the trash, then lit a match. The fire blew up his gas can, and he was badly burned.
_____
_____

3. Gwen was playing ball at school. When the ball rolled across the road, Gwen ran after it. She was struck by a truck, and had to spend several weeks in the hospital. _____
_____

4. Lucy's big brother sat Baby Lucy up on the table to play . Lucy fell off and got a bloody lip. _____
_____

5. Sarah was mowing the yard, and giving her little sister a ride on the mower. The little girl fell off and lost one of her legs in the mower blade. _____
_____

6. Baby Paul drowned when he was left alone in the bath tub. _____
_____

7. Five-year-old Carrie was using a sharp knife to open a package of hot dogs for herself. The knife slipped and stabbed her in the eye, making her eye blind.
_____
_____

8. Joseph was pretending to drive his father's car. The car rolled downhill, smashing into a tree.
_____
_____
_____

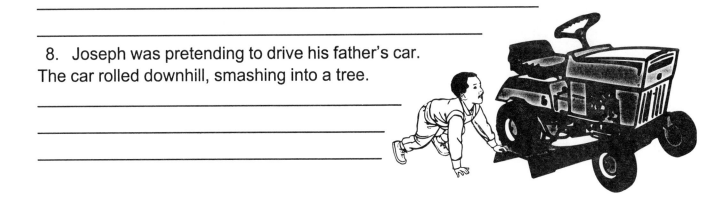

Being Thoughtful
Lesson 15

The basic idea behind all good manners is a simple one! Read Matthew 7:12, and copy the verse here: _____

_____

_____

How many examples of thoughtful behavior did *you* count in the story? _____

Why do you think the Miller family didn't experience any quarrels or fights on that day? _____

_____

_____

Look over your story again, and find three times that each of these children practiced the Golden Rule. List the things they did under each child's name:

Sharon

_____

_____

_____

Peter

_____

_____

_____

Timmy

_____

_____

_____

Now, try to think of three nice things *you* can do for others today to show thoughtfulness!

_____

_____

_____

Thinking of Others

We all live and work with other people, at home and at school. We will be happier and healthier if we learn to get along well with others! Getting along with others means thinking of how they feel, too. . . not just thinking of ourselves. Read each of the stories below, and tell how children like you could show thoughtfulness to the person in the story. Discuss your answers in class.

1. On Sunday morning, when all the children in your church go out to their Sunday School classes, you see two visiting children standing shyly in the stairway. They have no Sunday School book, and don't know which class to go with. What can you do? _____

_____

2. Your little sister has set up her doll dishes to have a tea party. Then the baby comes along and knocks them all down! She hit him, and now they are both crying. What should you do to make them both happy? _____

_____

3. Katie and Annie are two of your classmates. Katie said something that hurt Annie's feelings, and now Annie is upset. She is hiding behind the school building, and doesn't want to play with Katie. What could you do to help your friends?

_____

_____

4. Your friend Paul needs to go to the hospital tomorrow and have an operation. He is worried and a bit scared. What could you do or say to help Paul?

_____

_____

5. You would like to go outside and play ball, but your mother looks very busy and tired: the sink is piled high with dishes, the floor needs sweeping, the baby is crying, and Mom is trying to stir something on the stove. What should you do?

_____

_____

6. A friend gave you a candy bar at school today. You know it's your brother's favorite kind of candy! What should you do? _____

_____

7. Your bicycle is an old one, and your friend Jason just received a brand-new mountain bike for his birthday. You will soon be having a birthday, too, but your father has been very sick lately and your family has to pay a big hospital bill. Is this a good time to ask for a new bike? What should you do? _____

_____

_____

Check Yourself!

Be honest with yourself. How many of the "good manners" below are a habit with you? Read each one, and color the circle after the ones that you do. Now, see which good habits you need to work on!

I say "Good Morning" to my parents and teacher. ○

I say "Please" whenever I ask for something. ○

I say "Thank You " when something is given to me. ○

I say "I'm sorry!" if I have done something that hurts someone. ○

I let others choose first when treats are passed around. ○

I answer whenever someone calls me or speaks to me. ○

I come quickly when I am called. ○

I do not interrupt someone who is talking. I wait for my turn. ○

I say "Pardon?" instead of "Huh?" when I fail to hear. ○

I do not walk between two people who are talking to each other. ○

I cover my mouth when I cough or sneeze. ○

I never tap or pull on someone else to get their attention. ○

I pick up my toys or tools when I am finished using them. ○

I wait patiently for my turn when I am standing in line. ○

I hand sharp objects to others by giving them the handle. ○

I thank my mother or hostess when I have eaten a meal. ○

I ask permission before I borrow or use others' things. ○

I keep quiet when others are sleeping, studying, or talking on the phone. ○

I admire things that others have done or made, when they show them to me. ○

I do not open others' drawers, purses, or other private property. ○

I shake hands politely when I am introduced to an adult. ○

I try to help others have fun when I play a game. ○

I sit quietly in church and family worship. ○

I do not try to listen in when others are talking privately. ○

I try to think of kind, pleasant things to say to others. ○

48

RESPECT FOR PRIVACY
Lesson 16

In today's story, Laura tried to "find out" about three things that she shouldn't have:

She put her _____ against the _____ to listen to her _____ talking privately.

She flung open the _____ bedroom _____ to see what they were doing.

She climbed up to look into a _____ where her mother kept _____.

Take another look at pages 111 and 112 in your story, and fill in the blanks.

I Thess. 4:11 "Study to be _____ , and to _____ _____ _____ _____ , and to work with your _____ _____ as we commanded you."

Good Christian _____ means not trying to _____ in on _____ people's _____ _____ ; and not trying to _____ into other people's_____ . Also, there are rules about _____ private_____ , Do not _____ or look into other people's _____ or read other people's _____ unless they _____ or _____ _____ .

_____ _____ are a private matter between a student and his parents.

When someone is in their _____ or the_____ with the door shut, we must not go in without _____ .

Sometimes people need to be alone, for _____ and _____ .

Copy Sharon's rhyme on the lines below.

_____

_____

_____

_____

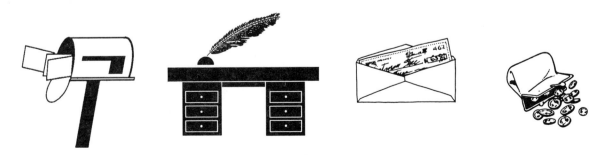

Let's talk about Poisons!

There are many chemicals which would be dangerous and harmful to your body if you ate them, breathed them, or rubbed them on your skin. Many of the things we use around the house have such chemicals in them. These things must be used carefully.

Suppose you are working on a model car or plane, and the strong smell of that model glue is all around you. What should you do? Open a window quickly! Or, go outside for some fresh air. The chemicals in that model glue are harmful to your body. If you breathe too much of them, you may get a painful headache, or get dizzy and sleepy.

There are many other substances we use which have dangerous chemicals in them. These things can be used safely, if you are careful to follow the rules and directions on their labels.

Here are some things that may be in your house, and the dangers of each:

Substance	Danger if not used properly
Bleach- such as Clorox	Will burn your skin if touched. Breathing fumes can damage lungs.
Whiteout fluid	Breathing too much of it will cause dizziness, sickness, and even death.
Oven-cleaning spray	Burns skin. Harmful or fatal if swallowed. Breathing fumes can burn lungs.
Rubbing Alcohol	Causes stomach upset and liver damage if swallowed. Too much will cause death.
Lye	Causes severe burns if it touches skin or eyes
Lighter Fluid	Will cause sickness or death if swallowed. May burn skin.
Mouse bait	Causes severe sickness or death if eaten or absorbed into skin.
Window-cleaning spray	Will cause temporary blindness and pain if sprayed into eyes.
Aspirin pills	Thins your blood if you take more than you should, causing bleeding inside and death.

Sometimes foolish people will purposely breathe the fumes from things like model glue and whiteout fluid. They think that it is fun to play dangerous games with their brains! Sniffing glue makes them feel drunk and dizzy, or very excited. They see *hallucinations*, or imaginary pictures in their minds. Some people have died because of doing this, and others have permanently destroyed their brains. It is a sin to abuse our bodies by doing anything like this. God wants us to take care of our bodies, because they are His.

Poisonous Plants

Many plants are also poisonous. House plants should be kept out of babies' reach, and you should never taste strange plants, mushrooms, or berries that you do not know are good to eat. Some plants, like poison ivy, have a poisonous oil on their leaves. Most people who touch the leaves get a very uncomfortable, itchy rash. Do you know what poison ivy looks like, so that you can safely avoid it?

Talk to your parents or grandparents, or look in an encyclopedia, and find the names of ten other plants that are poisonous. They may be house plants, yard plants, or wild plants. Write their names on the lines below. Try to find pictures of some of these plants in a seed catalog, and paste them beside the list!

Being Manly
Lesson 17

In today's story, Peter and Timmy learned some new things about the responsibilities of men and boys. A courteous boy is always appreciated!

When a man or boy goes to church, or when he is about to pray, he removes his hat or cap if he is wearing one. The reason for this rule is found in the Bible. Look up I Corinthians 11 and, copy verses 4 and 7 on the lines below:

_____

_____

_____

_____

_____

_____

It is polite and proper for boys and men to take off their caps when they meet a lady. Many people also expect boys and men to remove their caps as a sign of respect when they are at a funeral, or enter any public place such as a store or an elevator.

If a boy comes up to a _____ at the same time as a _____ or _____, he should _____ the door and let her go _____. He should offer to _____ heavy things for a woman or girl: and if there are not enough _____ to sit, he should _____ his _____ to a lady who needs one. A man or boy who shows _____ to ladies is taking his proper _____ in _____ creation. God intended _____ to be the _____, _____ and _____ for their _____ and society.

A Christian man will always behave like a _____. He will be _____ and _____ to those who are _____ and _____ than himself.

52

Review Time!

Do you remember?

1. Which one of the foods below is the best place to get calcium for your bones and teeth? Circle it.

  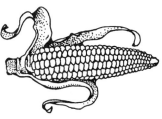

2. Circle the food that is most likely to give you vitamin C:

3. Which of these foods is rich in protein, to help you grow?

4. Circle the food that will give you energy, fiber, and vitamin E:

5. Circle the 3 foods that would be the wisest choices for a snack:

Match the Meanings

1. Diaphragm _____
2. Respiratory System _____
3. Epiglottis _____
4. Good Posture _____
5. Capillaries _____
6. Arteries _____
7. Saliva _____
8. Temperance _____
9. Esophagus _____
10. Small intestine _____
11. Large intestine _____
12. Hallucinations _____

a standing and sitting straight
b tiniest blood vessels
c carry fresh blood from your heart
d self-control
e "seeing" things that are not real
f lid that closes your windpipe
g muscle that helps you breathe
h breathing system
i liquid that helps digestion
j 20-foot tube where digestion is completed
k passage from throat to stomach
l collects wastes that can't be digested

True or False?

1. Whole wheat bread is better for your body than white bread. _____
2. Working or playing hard takes more oxygen than sitting still. _____
3. Coughing squeezes air out of your stomach. _____
4. It is healthier to breathe through your mouth, not your nose. _____
5. Swimming during a thunder storm is dangerous. _____
6. Swimming alone is the safest way. _____
7. Your body holds about 10 quarts of blood. _____
8. Veins are the blue blood vessels under your skin, and arteries are red. _____
9. A grown-up's heart beats faster than a child's heart. _____
10. When you hand someone a sharp tool, give them the handle. _____
11. Lots of aspirin is good for you. _____
12. Most house plants are good to eat. _____

54

Being a Lady
Lesson 18

1. Can you find the hidden treasure? Open your Bible to 1 Peter 3:4, and find out what God says the ornament of a lady should be! Copy the last half of verse 4 on these lines: _____

_____

_____

2. Look at page 124 in your story book, and complete the sentences:

"In like manner also, that _____ adorn themselves in _____

_____, with _____ and _____; not with _____

hair, or _____, or _____, or costly _____; But, which

becometh women professing _____, with _____

_____."

God wants women and _____ to be _____, _____ and

_____. We should be _____ to show off our bodies in an

_____ _____. A true _____ _____ doesn't

need to _____ herself with _____ and fancy _____. A

Christian _____ is _____ because she is _____,

_____ and _____.

3. The Bible says that a lady will speak wisely, gently, and kindly. Look up Proverbs 31:26, and write the verse here: _____

_____

_____

4. It is not lady-like to be bossy, boastful, or to show off. Look up Philippians 2:3, and copy it here:

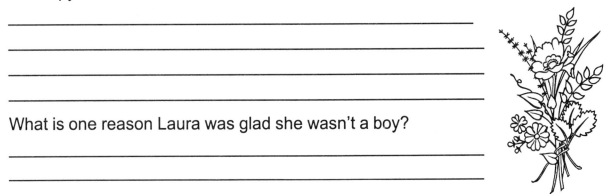

_____

_____

_____

_____

What is one reason Laura was glad she wasn't a boy?

_____

_____

Our Clothes

Our clothes are to cover and protect our bodies. The clothing we wear has a lot to do with our health! Clothes help to protect our bodies from injury and from germs. When your clothes fit well, they are comfortable. They do not pinch or bind your body anywhere.

Clothes protect your body from the weather. In hot weather, clothes protect you from the rays of the sun. Sunlight has *ultraviolet rays*, which will damage skin if you receive too much of them. Ultraviolet rays will give you a sunburn, and if you get many sunburns you may also get skin cancer.

Some people think summer weather is too hot to wear clothes! They like to go around nearly naked in the summertime. This is not wise or healthy.

One of the hottest climates in the world is the desert country of the Middle East where Arabs live. The Arabs, who have been living there ever since the days of Abraham and Ishmael, know how to dress for hot weather! They cover their bodies, and even their heads, with long, loose, flowing garments.

In the wintertime, we wear heavier clothes to keep our body heat from escaping. Becoming too chilled is hard on your body, and when your body is weakened you will become sick more easily. Much of your body heat is lost through your head, if you do not wear a hat, cap, or scarf in cold weather. It is also important to keep your feet warm and dry! Wearing several layers of warm clothing can keep your body warm better than just wearing one heavy coat.

When we must go out in the rain, we should wear waterproof clothing and boots. If you do get wet, take off your wet clothes and shoes as soon as possible! Wearing wet clothes is hard on your body.

God wants us to wear clothes that cover our bodies modestly. We also want to be clean and neat in our appearance, to the glory of God! Boys should keep their shirts buttoned, and tucked neatly into their pants. Girls should keep their dresses down and not show their underwear or their bare legs. We should not follow silly fads, such as wearing clothes that are torn on purpose or leaving our shoelaces dragging loose.

Clothing Habits

Color the picture after each good clothing habit that you make practice of following! Which ones might you need to work on improving?

I dress warmly in cold weather.

I protect myself from the sun's rays.

I change my clothes when I come home from school.

I hang up my clothes.

I put my dirty clothes into the laundry.

I show my clothes to my mother if they need mending.

I keep my clothes modestly buttoned and zipped.

I keep my shoes clean and neatly tied.

I keep my clothes neatly folded and close my drawers.

I keep dry on rainy days.

I wear clean, comfortable night clothes.

When We Go Visiting
Lesson 19

Think it over!

1. Which one of the Millers was the most excited about visiting the Bender family? _____

2. What do you suppose are some good rules for shaking hands courteously with an adult, as Peter and Timmy did in the beginning of your story? (Hint: which hand should you use? What should your eyes do? Is there anything you ought to say?)

_____

_____

3. Why do you think Peter told Frank that Freddy should come along with the older boys?_____

_____

4. Write a rule for good manners that Sharon practiced on page 126. _____

_____

5. Which good health rule did Sharon use before she poured water? _____

_____

6. What did the Miller children remember to do after the meal? _____

_____

7. Write the rule for good manners that Dad Miller told Timmy on page 128: ____

_____

8. Copy the rule that Laura learned, from the same page: _____

_____

9. What is the right thing to do when you damage an item that belongs to another person? _____

_____

10. What does Proverbs 25:17 mean? Explain. _____

_____

11. What are some courteous things to say when you leave a friend's house?____

_____

_____

12. What is the best way to have an enjoyable visit at a friend's house?

_____

_____

Setting the Table

Help Sharon set the table for a company meal!
Find 25 different things in the puzzle below that you might use when you set a table. As you find each one, cross it off the bottom of the page.

I	A	B	M	D	B	O	W	L	C	J	T
A	C	D	U	E	I	F	G	H	N	E	O
I	L	E	G	L	A	S	S	F	O	L	S
P	I	T	C	H	E	R	H	O	O	L	A
J	K	L	S	A	U	C	E	R	P	Y	L
T	O	O	T	H	P	I	C	K	S	M	T
N	A	O	A	W	A	T	E	R	P	R	S
Q	R	B	B	S	T	K	N	I	F	E	H
N	U	P	L	A	T	E	E	V	W	T	A
A	X	Y	E	E	Z	A	B	R	C	T	K
P	L	A	C	E	M	A	T	C	D	U	E
K	E	F	L	O	W	E	R	S	U	B	R
I	F	G	O	R	E	T	T	A	L	P	G
N	H	I	T	E	A	P	O	T	J	K	O
A	B	C	H	A	I	R	L	M	N	O	T

TABLE	CHAIR	TOOTHPICKS
GLASS	BUTTER	TABLECLOTH
PITCHER	SPOON	BOWL
JELLY	NAPKIN	MUG
DISH	FLOWERS	ICE
KNIFE	FORK	PLACEMAT
CUP	WATER	PLATE
SAUCER	TEAPOT	SALTSHAKER
PLATTER		

All Kinds of Guests

How many of these people would *you* like to have as a guest in your home? If you think the people in the story are being courteous guests, draw a smiling face in the circle after the story. If they do not sound like nice guests to have, draw a frowning face.

1. "Here's a ball!" Tommy cheered, pulling it out of the Miller's toybox. Tommy and his brother Jerry were soon bouncing the ball all around the Millers' living room, making Mama look anxiously at her plants on the windowsill.

2. "Don't give me any of that casserole. I don't think I'll like it, " Sarah whispered loudly to her mother as she sat at the Millers' table.

3. "I'd like to play one of the games in that cabinet," Sally whispered to her sister. "Shall we just get one out?" "No, let's ask first if we may open the cabinet." said Cindy. "That would be more polite."

4. Keith and Paul sat quietly at the table, waiting until everyone finished eating. After everyone *was* done, the grown-ups still sat, talking on and on! Finally Keith whispered to his father, "May we children be excused?" "Ask Mr. Miller," his father replied. Dad Miller smiled at the boy, as he asked politely, "May be excused, please?"

5. When Jessie visited the Millers, she carefully cleaned all the snow from her shoes before she walked in the door.

6. Little Sam was very mean to Baby Beth when he visited the Millers. He pulled her hair, grabbed toys from her, and hit her on the head with a toy truck. Sam's parents pretended not to notice.

7. "It's almost time to go home," said Matthew's father. "Matthew and Mark, you must pick up all the toys and put them back into the Millers' toybox."

8. When Joe came to spend the afternoon with his friend Peter, he did not speak to Peter's parents at all! He walked past Dad Miller without answering his "Hello, Joe!" and ignored Dad's outstretched hand.

Table Manners
Lesson 20

How much do you remember? Finish the Millers' mealtime rules:

1. Wash your _____ and _____ your _____ before you come to the _____.
2. When _____, close your _____ and _____ your _____. Keep your _____ in your _____ during prayer.
3. After ____ _____ _____ to _____, pass it on to your _____.
4. Take _____ speaking. Talk about _____ things, and do not _____ _____.
5. Never _____ or _____ about the _____.
6. _____ your _____ _____, with your mouth _____.
7. Do not _____ your _____, or _____ with your mouth _____.
8. Do not _____ until you swallow your _____.
9. Stay at the _____ until everyone is _____ and has been _____.
10. If we have Christian courtesy, we will not _____ the _____ or the _____ for ourselves!

The words of your memory verses are in alphabetical order here. Unscramble and write them on the lines.

> another brethren come eat for my one tarry
> to together when wherefore ye

_____

_____

> all do do drink eat glory God of or or the
> therefore to whatsoever whether wherefore ye

_____

_____

First Aid for Emergencies

An *emergency* is an accident that calls for immediate action. *First Aid* is the care given to an injured person right away. For a small injury, such as splinters or nosebleeds, first aid may be all that is needed. In case of a serious injury, first aid may help save a life! Would you know exactly what to do for first aid in each of these emergencies?

Choking Choking happens if some food or other object gets stuck in a person's larynx, the opening to the windpipe. If the person cannot cough up the object, and cannot breathe, they will soon die from lack of oxygen. Here is how you can help: stand behind the person who is choking. Wrap both your arms around their waist. Make a fist with one of your hands, with the thumb side against the person's stomach just above their navel. Place your other hand around the fist, and press upward as hard as you can with both hands together. This should force air from the person's lungs hard enough to push out the object that is stuck. You may need to repeat this if it does not work the first time.

Severe Bleeding If a person has a wound that was bad enough to injure large blood vessels, they may bleed until a dangerous amount of blood is lost. To stop the bleeding, put a pad of clean cloth over the wound and press it until the blood stops flowing, then wind strips of cloth around the pad to hold it there. If someone's arm or leg is bleeding rapidly, raise it up and prop it with a pillow. This will let gravity help to slow the bleeding. The injured person must lie still while someone else calls for help.

Nosebleeds If someone has a nosebleed, tell them to sit down with their head straight up or tilted slightly back, and pinch the nostrils gently together with a wet handkerchief or paper towel to help the blood *clot,* or thicken.

Stings and Bites If you are stung by a honey bee, make sure the stinger is removed from your skin by carefully scraping it away with your fingernail or a knife or card. Do not squeeze the sack on the end of the stinger. Use a cold wet cloth or an ice pack to relieve the swelling and pain. Taking 500 units of Vitamin C may help to keep swelling down. If you feel sick or have trouble breathing after being stung, lie down and keep still while another person goes for help. Anyone who has been bitten by a snake should lie still while someone else goes for help immediately.

Burns Burns are very painful. If you or someone else has been burned, soak the burned area in a clean, cold water to take away the pain. Then spread the burned skin with antibiotic ointment and cover it with clean bandages. Never break open a blister. If a burn is very deep or covers large areas of a person's body, go to the doctor quickly.

Broken bones A person with a broken bone should be kept from moving, so that the jagged ends of bone do not make the damage worse. Put a coat, sweater or blanket around the injured person to keep him warm, and call for help.

Splinters When you must remove a splinter, sterilize the needle or tweezers before you use it by dropping it in alcohol to kill any germs on it. Pinch the area around the splinter with your left thumb and finger as you work, to make it feel numb and bring the splinter into view. After the splinter is out, pour peroxide on the wound, blot dry, and apply antibiotic ointment and a band-aid.

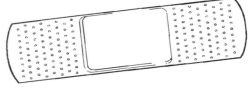

What Would You Do?

After you have studied the First Aid guide on page 59, read each of these stories and write down what you would do in each emergency.

1. You are out in the yard with your little sister, and suddenly she begins to scream. You see a red and white spot on her foot, with a tiny black stinger still in the center of the spot. _____

_____

_____

2. You are playing a game at school, and accidentally bump your friend's nose, making it begin to bleed. _____

_____

_____

3. Your father cuts his leg with the chainsaw when you are in the woods together. Blood is gushing from the wound. _____

_____

_____

_____

4. You are eating lunch outdoors with your friends at school, when suddenly one of your friends stands up. His face looks terrified, and is turning a strange color. He cannot speak, but he looks at you and waves his arms in panic. _____

_____

_____

_____

5. You were baking cookies, and took hold of the hot cookie sheet without thinking of protecting your hand. Now your hand is red and hurts terribly. _____

_____

_____

_____

6. Your brother slipped and fell out of a tree! Now he is lying on the ground groaning, and his left leg looks like it is bent into a strange position. _____

_____

_____

_____

7. You were running around in the hayloft, and got a big splinter in your foot! Your mother usually takes out splinters for you, but now she is not at home.

_____

_____

_____

Prejudice
Lesson 21

Did you understand? Write *True* or *False* after each sentence.

1. Philip thought the visiting family were "weird" people. _____
2. Dad Miller was pleased to hear Philip say this. _____
3. Prejudice is a pleasant attitude._____
4. Mocking others is always an ugly thing to do. _____
5. Timmy obeyed his father and treated the visitors courteously. _____
6. David, the black boy, was not nice. _____
7. God will reward those who are kind to handicapped people. _____
8. All Christians are adopted into God's family. _____
9. The color of a person's skin shows what he is like inside. _____
10. Prejudice means treating people unfairly. _____
11. The Bible says partiality and prejudice are wrong. _____
12. God wants us to have "respect of persons" for rich people. _____
13. God made all nations of one blood. _____
14. Moses' wife was an Ethiopian. _____
15. God rebuked Moses for marrying a dark-skinned woman. _____
16. Every human being is a valuable individual, made in God's image. _____

   In the last paragraph of your story, you may read about three famous persons who were handicapped in some way, and yet made a valuable contribution to people everywhere. Tell in your own words what each of these famous people did.

Fanny Crosby

_____

_____

Helen Keller

_____

_____

Thomas Edison

_____

_____

Prejudice or Tolerance?

Prejudice is jumping to conclusions about people and treating them unfairly. *Tolerance* is the ability to accept others who are different from yourself, and treat them with courtesy. Write "TT" for "Tolerant Timmy," or "PP" for "Prejudiced Philip," in the space after each of the little stories below!

1.   When Ruth, the tall new girl, stepped up to take her turn at batting the ball, all the fifth-grade boys groaned. "She won't be any good," Thomas predicted. "Girls can never hit a ball very far!"   _____

2.   Mrs. Smith was shopping at K-Mart. She noticed that the clerk at cash register number 2 was a black woman, and the clerk at number 3 was a white woman. Mrs. Smith took her cart to cash register number 3 because she does not like to talk to black people.   _____

3.   Willie went home for supper with his friend Carlos. Carlos' mother served several kinds of Spanish foods which Willie had never eaten before. Willie politely tried some of everything and found out that he enjoyed the new foods very much!   _____

4.   When the visiting minister stepped up to the pulpit, Mervin slumped down into his seat and frowned. *He's old, and bald, and just look at that weird kind of suit he's wearing!,* Mervin thought to himself. *I just know his sermon is going to be boring!*   _____

5.   In Jeremy's church, there are black families, white families and Spanish families. All the children go to school together, and Jeremy's friends don't worry about the different colors of their faces.   _____

6.   Jewel grumbled and complained when her mother told her that she had invited the Martin family for Sunday dinner. "I hate it when they come, because of Sarah," said Jewel. "I don't like to play with retarded children."   _____

7.   Lisa and Laurie were upset when they learned their new schoolteacher was going to be a man. "School won't be fun anymore!" said Lisa. "Man teachers are sure to be mean and nasty," said Laurie.   _____

8.   When Franklin's family moved to Romania for mission work, Franklin was sorry to leave his friends behind, but he was excited and happy too. "I can hardly wait to make some Romanian friends!" he said.   _____

The Porter's Mistake

Thomas Edison's school teacher made an embarrassing mistake! When Edison was a boy, his teacher said that he was too stupid to learn anything. Just imagine how that teacher would have felt, years later, if she learned of all the important inventions Edison made! That teacher missed a great opportunity by refusing to teach Thomas Edison.

Another time, there was a porter in a train station in the city of Washington, DC who missed an opportunity because he jumped to conclusions. An elderly black man in plain shabby clothes stepped off the train that morning, and looked around him in a bewildered way. Crowds of people were hurrying through the station, going this way and that, and nobody paid any attention to the lonely old man with a homemade box under his arm.

The little old man finally managed to stop one of the porters. He asked him a question about where to go, but the porter rudely brushed him away. "Sorry, Pop," said the red-capped porter, " I don't have time to give you any directions now. We're all trying to find a great scientist who's coming in on this train from Alabama!"

That busy porter was making a big mistake. Can you guess who that shabby, stooped old black man was? The great scientist from Alabama, George Washington Carver, was right under the porter's nose... but he missed him, because he didn't take time to be courteous!

George Washington Carver was born in slavery, but he became one of the greatest scientists the world has ever known. There are many interesting books about this great Christian scientist. Ask your parents or teacher to help you find one to read.

Thankful Puzzle
Lesson 22

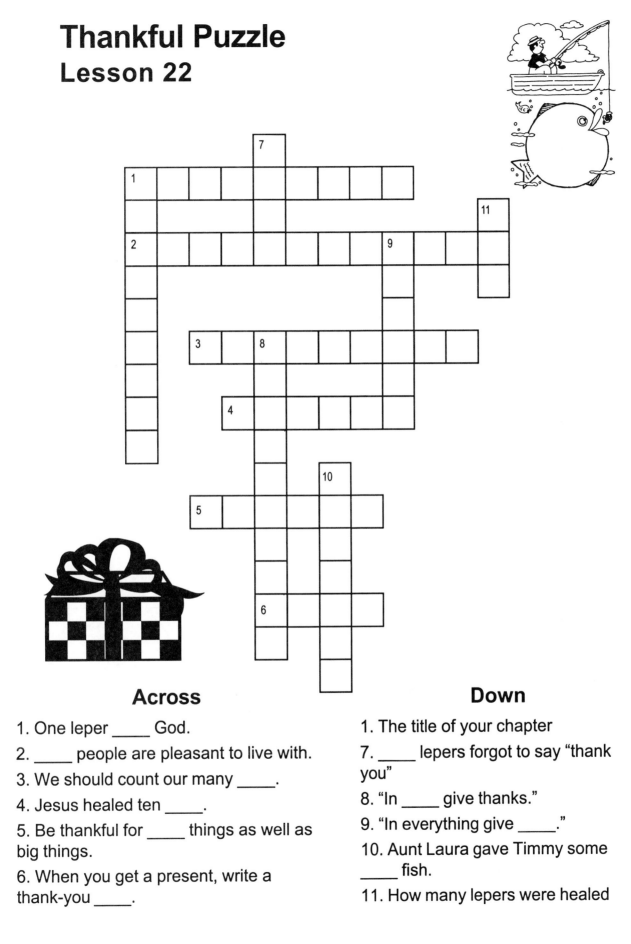

Across

1. One leper ____ God.

2. ____ people are pleasant to live with.

3. We should count our many ____.

4. Jesus healed ten ____.

5. Be thankful for ____ things as well as big things.

6. When you get a present, write a thank-you ____.

Down

1. The title of your chapter

7. ____ lepers forgot to say "thank you"

8. "In ____ give thanks."

9. "In everything give ____."

10. Aunt Laura gave Timmy some ____ fish.

11. How many lepers were healed

Writing a Thank-You Note

Think of a gift someone has given you, or a gift you would like to get! Write a thank-you note on the lines below.

_____

_____

_____

_____

_____

_____

_____

_____

_____

_____

_____

_____

Thanking God

How often do you thank God for His many blessings to you? Count some blessings you are thankful for today, and write the list here. Make a pretty border for the page by drawing and coloring small pictures of some of the things you are thankful for.

_____

_____

_____

_____

_____

_____

_____

_____

_____

_____

_____

_____

_____

_____

_____

_____

_____

When We Go to Town
Lesson 23

1. Why did the Millers fasten their seat belts? Give 2 reasons: _____
_____
_____

2. Why should children stay close to their parents in town? _____
_____

3. What are "shoplifters"? _____

4. Why should children not handle the goods in a store? _____
_____

5. How can Christian people be "a light to the world" in public? _____
_____

6. Name 3 ways we could bring shame to the Name of Christ by our actions in public._____
_____
_____

7. How did Timmy get lost in the store? _____
_____
_____

8. Name the four best kinds of people for children to ask help from if they are lost: _____ _____ _____ _____

9. Be sure you know your _____ full names, your _____ and your _____ number.

10. What did Mama say when a strange lady admired her beautiful children?
_____
_____

11. What were the Millers thankful for when they prayed? _____
_____

12. Copy Phillippians 2:15 here: _____
_____
_____
_____

The Reasons for the Rules

There are Bible verses on the left side of the page. Draw a line between each verse and the rule on the right side that best matches its lesson.

1. Abstain from all appearance of evil. I Thessalonians 5:22

2. Let every soul be subject unto the higher powers. For... the powers that be are ordained of God. Romans 13:1

3. Be kindly affectioned one to another with brotherly love; in honour preferring one another. Romans 12:10

4. A false balance is abomination unto the Lord, but a just weight is His delight. Proverbs 11:1

5. Thou shalt not steal. Exodus 20:15

6. My son, forget not my law, but let thine heart keep my commandments: for length of days, and long life, and peace, shall they add to thee. Proverbs 3:1&2

7. Whatsoever ye do, do all to the glory of God. 1 Corinthians 10:31

8. And if ye salute your brethren only, what do ye more than others? Mathew 5:47

A. We must wait politely for our turn to be served in a store or other public place. Courteous people allow others to go first.

B. Never take things without paying for them.

C. We must be careful to not even *look* like we are going to steal something!

D. Christians will obey the laws and the policemen.

E. We must be careful to behave properly in public, so we can be a good testimony in everything.

F. Never try to cheat when you are buying or selling! Weigh, measure, and count things honestly.

H. Be polite and friendly to everyone. Smile at others and return their greetings, even if you do not know them.

G. Staying close to your parents, and obeying their instructions, will keep you safe.

What Would You Do?

What would be the best thing for each of these children to do? Read each story and tell how you think the story should end. Discuss your answers in class.

1. When Sarah's mother sent her to the store to buy 2 loaves of bread, Sarah noticed that the clerk only charged her enough money for one loaf. *I could use the extra money to buy something for myself!* Sarah thought. *But maybe I should tell the lady about her mistake and pay the rest.* What should Sarah do?

_____

_____

2. Paul was waiting for his father by the door of the store, when a man he did not know came up to him. "Sonny, I've lost my little dog," the man told Paul. "Will you please come outside in the parking lot and help me look for him?" Paul knew that children should never go anywhere with a stranger, but it looked like he really did need help. What could Paul do? _____

_____

3. As Laurie was riding her bike, she saw a lady's purse lying beside the road. *How can I ever find out whose purse this is?* Laurie wondered. *Maybe I should just keep it!* _____

_____

4. Matthew wanted to buy a vase for his mother's birthday. As he was picking up the different vases in the store, to decide which was the prettiest, he accidently broke one! *If I hide the broken vase behind these other ones, nobody will know,* Matthew thought. *But what would be the right thing to do?* _____

_____

_____

5. "Thank you," said the clerk with a smile when Jason paid for his father's nails. "Have a good day now!" What should Jason say in return? _____

_____

6. Beth Ann unwrapped a stick of gum and popped it into her mouth, then looked around for a place to put the empty wrapper. "The trash can is so far away!" Beth Ann groaned. "I could just wad up my gum wrapper and drop it on the pavement. . . it's such a little thing!" What should she do?

_____

_____

Habits
Lesson 24

What is a habit? Look back at your lesson story, and fill in the missing words.

"A habit is a _____ pattern. An _____ which we have _____ over and over until it _____ part of _____, and can be _____ without conscious _____. Good _____ make our life _____ and more _____, but _____ _____ can cause a lot of _____!"

What was wrong with Brother Ken's kerosene lamp? _____

_____

_____

The lamp reminded Brother Ken of a person whose _____ _____ spoiled his _____ and _____.

Write Ecclesiastes 10:1 on these lines: _____

_____

_____

_____

Everybody has habits. Habits are the things that we are used to doing, so that we do them without thinking. Some habits are good, and some are not good! How can we change our bad habits? It is not easy to break a bad habit, because we have "worn a path" in our lives for that habit by doing it over and over again. The best way to get rid of a bad habit is to *replace* it with a habit that is good.

Joe has a bad habit of dropping his lunchbox, coat, and books on the floor when he comes home from school. If he practices every day, he can replace that bad habit with the good habit of putting his things in their places!

"Habits are _____ to _____, and easiest to _____, when you are _____! So if you are reminded of any _____ habit you have, begin right away to _____ that habit."

Replacing Bad Habits

The children in these stories have bad habits. Think of a good habit that each child should use, to replace their bad habits. Discuss your answers.

1. Lewis has the habit of saying everything too loudly. _____
_____

2. When Ruthie's fingernails are long or uneven, she chews them off.
_____
_____

3. Janet picks her nose. _____
_____

4. Caleb has a habit of interrupting; he does not like to wait for his turn to speak.
_____
_____

5. Mervin's older brother sucks at his teeth. _____
_____

6. Sometimes when Alice has to cough or sneeze, she does it right at other people._____
_____

7. Jason wipes his runny nose on his hands, and smears his hands on his clothing. _____
_____

8. Paul stuffs his mouth so full when he eats, that food sometimes dribbles out at the corners. _____
_____

9. When Mary Ann bats the softball, she throws the bat aside as she runs to first base. _____
_____

10. Lois is usually the last one in her family to be ready to go, and the others must wait for her. _____
_____

11. Lavon's pajamas are always lost when he wants to get ready for bed.
_____
_____

12. Sally hardly ever brushes her teeth. _____
_____

Your Brain and Your Habits

Your brain looks something like a big, wrinkly flower on a stem. The top part of your brain, the *cerebrum*, is the thinking part of your brain. This is where information that you learn is stored in your memory bank. This is where you reason and make decisions.

At the base of your brain is the lower part called the *cerebellum*. This part handles the things that happen automatically, like your breathing. Your cerebellum also helps you keep your balance.

Your spinal cord is the "stem" of your brain. When you touch a hot stove and your hand quickly jerks away; this *reflex* action was controlled in your spinal cord. Reflexes are quick responses that you don't even take time to think about in the upper part of your brain!

Memory is an important part of your brain. Doctors are not even sure how memory works, but we thank God for it! What would it be like if you could not remember anything? Each morning you would have to search all through your house for the breakfast table. When it was time to go home from church, you would not know which of the men and women were *your* parents. You would need to learn how to tie your shoes all over again, everyday! School work would be totally impossible.

Memory allows us to form habits, so that things are easier to do. Habits save a lot of time. Try this experiment: number a paper from one to twenty. Count how many seconds it takes to print your name twenty times. Now, on the other side of the paper, write your name backwards twenty times, while you time yourself again! Which took longer?

Let's form *good* habits, and store up *good* memories in our brains!

1. Peter Miller
2. Peter Miller
3. Peter Miller

1. Rellim Retep
2. Rellim Retep
3. Rellim Retep

Telephone Manners
Lesson 25

Fill in the blanks to complete each rule for good telephone manners from your story.

1.   Speaking on the telephone is like other speech; it must be _____, _____ and _____. We must study what is _____ to say, and speak _____ that. The telephone is not a _____, but an important _____.

2.   Speak in a _____ tone of voice on the telephone: do not _____ or _____. Don't talk too _____ either, and try to speak in a pleasant voice!

3.   It is not nice to call at _____ times, or too _____ in the morning, or late at _____. Never speak too _____; we need to allow _____ to use the telephone.

4.   When you need to take a message, carefully write down the _____ and _____ _____ of the person who called, and their message.

5.   When you have dialled the wrong number, _____ politely and _____ hang up the receiver.

6.   Never try to _____ in on others' phone calls. Why? _____
_____
_____

7.   Never play _____ with the telephone. Prank calls are illegal and annoying.

8.   If we always think of others, of their _____ and of their _____, our telephone manners will be correct.

Remember Sharon's friend Janet? List three mistakes that she made in her telephone use:

_____
_____
_____

The First Telephone

The telephone was invented by Alexander Graham Bell, a Scotsman who had come to the United States in 1871. Alexander Bell was a teacher of deaf people, and he was very interested in finding a way to help them hear. He spent his evenings experimenting with spring steel reeds, trying to send messages over the wires. On March tenth, 1876, he finally succeeded in speaking words over a telephone wire!

Bell's telephone could not help his deaf pupils to hear as he hoped it might. But his invention has become an important tool that helps people communicate with one another. We now can speak with people on the other side of the world, and hear them speaking as clearly as if they were in our own house!

When we speak into a telephone receiver, the sound waves from our mouth strike against an aluminum disk, causing it to vibrate the same way that the air molecules are vibrating. Electrons carrying the rhythm of those molecules are sent through the wires to the other person's receiver, where another diaphragm disk picks up the electrons to reproduce the voice.

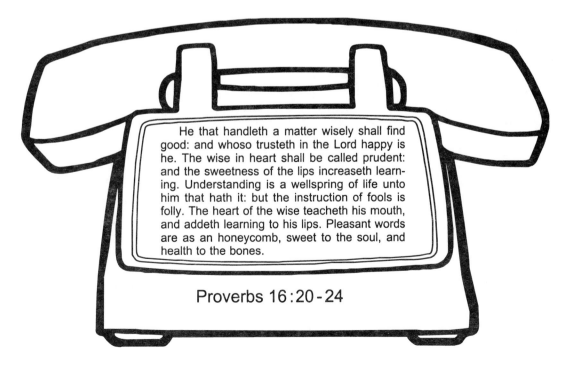

He that handleth a matter wisely shall find good: and whoso trusteth in the Lord happy is he. The wise in heart shall be called prudent: and the sweetness of the lips increaseth learning. Understanding is a wellspring of life unto him that hath it: but the instruction of fools is folly. The heart of the wise teacheth his mouth, and addeth learning to his lips. Pleasant words are as an honeycomb, sweet to the soul, and health to the bones.

Proverbs 16:20-24

As You Grow

What makes you grow, and why do different people grow at different rates? Do you ever wonder why the other children in your class are larger or smaller than you?

Growth happens when tiny cells in our bodies divide. One cell becomes two cells, each of those two divide into two more cells, and so on. Some parts of you grow faster than others. Your brain is nearly full-grown by the age of five years, but your bones will keep on growing until you are almost twenty years old. Your hair, fingernails, and toenails will keep growing as you live!

Three things control the speed of your growth and the size to which you will grow. One is the *pituitary gland* in your brain. This gland sends out growth *hormones.* When the pituitary gland sends out more growth hormones, you grow faster. When these hormones slow down, your growth also is slower.

Your growth is also controlled by *heredity.* Heredity means the ways in which you are like your parents, grandparents, and other people in your family. If your parents and grandparents are tall people, you will tend to be like they are. If one of your parents or grandparents is very short, you may also be a fairly short adult.

Our health also can influence growth. If you are a healthy child who gets enough sleep, exercise, sunlight, and good food, especially foods that are rich in protein and calcium, you do not need to worry about your growth.

You and your friends will all go through about the same stages in growth, and go through these normal stages in about the same order. The ages at which you reach each stage, though, may be a little different! Do not worry if you reach one stage of growth a little sooner or later than your friends. The slow-growing children will catch up with the faster ones, and in a few years you will be more alike. God made each of us to grow in our own way! We must not worry about our differences, or tease others about their differences.

| Martha | Regina | Robert | Dale |

These children were all ten-year-olds, from a class I taught. All 4 grew up to be healthy adults.

In God's House
Lesson 26

True, or False?

1. During the church service is a good time to chat with your friends. ____
2. Children your age should help sing in church. ____
3. When Laura paid attention and listened, it was easier to sit still. ____
4. Going out of the church services to get drinks is a good idea. ____
5. It is not courteous to stare at people sitting behind you. ____
6. Noisy babies should be carried out of church services. ____
7. Going in and out of church services makes it hard for others to worship. ____
8. We should look at the speaker, or worship leader, and listen. ____
9. Keeping our eyes shut during the prayer helps us to pray reverently. ____
10. Boys and girls should draw pictures in church services. ____
11. Chewing gum in church is the polite thing to do. ____
12. It is not important to get to church on time. ____
13. People who come into church late ought to sit up front. ____
14. Church services are a good place to take a nap. ____
15. We should be thankful for the privilege of worshipping together. ____

????????????????? Can you guess these riddles ????????????????

I am a dangerous, forbidden object in some countries of the world. I am a "library" of 66 different books. I am one of the first things people think of taking along when they go to church. What am I?

_____

I am not a *thing*, but it is easy for others to see if you have brought me along to church or not. You should be afraid to come before God without me. I have nine letters, and begin with the letter "R". What am I?

_____

Water

It should not be necessary for you to walk out of a church service just to take a drink. Drinking water, though, *is* very important! Your body needs a lot of water. Nearly two-thirds of a person's body *is* water. Your brain is 85% water, which means nearly all of it! Even your bones are 25%, or one-fourth water.

Drinking plenty of water is necessary for good health. Adults should drink six to eight glasses full of water or other liquids each day for their bodies to work at their best. Boys and girls your age should drink about six glasses full every day. When the weather is hot and you are working or playing hard, your body needs even more.

Milk and fruit juices can be counted as part of your daily six glasses, but you should not drink a lot of sweet drinks such as soda pop or Kool-aid. Even fruit juices can be bad for your body if you drink too much of them, because the extra sugar they contain may be too much for your body to handle. Drinking plain, clear water is best.

It is not a good idea to drink a lot of water during a meal. Drinking too much while you are eating will make it harder for your stomach to digest the food. Milk may be drunk with a meal, though, since it is actually a food and needs to be digested, too.

How many glasses of water and other liquids do *you* drink in one day? Try to keep track! Here are two rows of six glasses, one for today and one for tomorrow. Color one glass for each glassful you drink. Each time you drink a glass of water, color one of the glasses blue. Color a glass white or pale yellow for each glass of milk you drink, and red or orange for fruit juice. Try to fill all six glasses each day!

Your Posture

Your *posture* is how you hold your body when you are sitting, standing, or walking. People who have good posture stand straight, without slumping. They lift up their feet when they walk, instead of shuffling or slouching.

Good posture is important for good health! If your body is slumped over, your heart and lungs will be crowded inside your chest and not be able to work properly. Boys and girls should practice good posture while they are growing up, so that their bones can grow straight and strong.

Good posture also helps you be able to sit, stand, or work for a longer time without becoming tired. Sitting properly includes letting feet rest flat on the floor. Sit erect with your stomach pulled in. In church, you should always sit up straight with your shoulders back and your face turned toward the speaker or worship leader. Never hunch down with your elbows in your lap.

When you stand and walk, stand tall! Your head should be up, your shoulders level, and your tummy pulled in. You do not want to hold your body stiffly; be straight, yet relaxed.

Practice the habit of good posture! Good posture makes you look and feel better.

Look at the pictures of boys and girls on this page, and color the ones who have good posture.

Honoring Our Parents
Lesson 27

Choose the word that belongs in each blank, and put it into the right place in the puzzle.

1. "Thou shalt rise up before the ____ head."   H _ _ _ _ _
2. We must ____ our parents   O _ _ _ _
3. Be ____ for godly parents!   _ _ _ N _ _ _ _
4. ____ keeps us safe from many troubles and dangers. O _ _ _ _ _ _ _ _ _ _
5. Speak to your parents with ____.   R _ _ _ _ _ _ _

6. Respecting parents is one of the ____ commandments. T _ _
7. ____ thy father and mother.   H _ _ _ _
8. ____ people need to show respect to their elders.   Y _ _ _ _ _

9. Honouring parents is the ____ commandment with a promise. F _ _ _ _ _
10. That thou mayest live long on the ____.   _ A _ _ _
11. Ask your parents questions ____ and respectfully. _ _ _ _ T _ _ _
12. Obey ____ and not grudgingly.   _ H _ _ _ _ _ _ _ _
13. Honour you parents ____ though. . .   E _ _ _
14. . . .they are not ____.   _ _ R _ _ _ _ _

15. Being respectful helps us live in ____.   _ _ A _ _
16. Most good ____ come from the Bible.   _ _ N _ _ _ _
17. ____ requires children to honour parents.   _ _ D

18. The ____ told a lot of good stories   M _ _ _ _ _ _ _
19. We should ____ when we have been disrespectful   _ _ O _ _ _ _ _ _
20. ____ up when you meet an older person.   _ T _ _ _ _
21. ____ 6:1-3 is our Bible reference.   _ _ H _ _ _ _ _
22. You will be ____ if you honour your parents.   _ _ E _ _ _ _
23. "Children, obey your ____!"   _ _ R _ _ _ _

82

Who Honored their Parents?

Read each story below and decide whether the children showed respect for their parents. If they honored their parents, draw a smiling face in the circle after the story. If they did not, draw a frowning face.

1. Miriam's parents did not want her to wade in the creek without permission. When Miriam's friends were at her farm on Sunday afternoon, they all ran into the creek and waded and spashed each other, but Miriam stayed on the grass and watched. ◯

2. Timmy saw an old man with a cane walking slowly up to the door of his church. Remembering what his parents had taught him about good manners, Timmy ran over to open the door for the man. ◯

3. "My dad was awfully mad at my brother yesterday," Jerry laughed as he told his friend Paul. "You should have seen how red his face got!" ◯

4. Rosie and Mary were supposed to fold all the clean clothes. Mom did not say they had to put the clothes away, but Rosie and Mary did that, too, before they went out to play. ◯

5. "Sam, you know Mom doesn't want you to throw balls in the house!" his brother Jim reminded. "I'm not *throwing* the ball. I'm only *kicking* it," said Sam. ◯

6. Beth made a little card for her parents. She thanked them for being good Christian parents, and for taking care of her. She put the card on her parents' bed for a surprise. ◯

7. When Joseph was given a candy bar at school, he decided to save it for his father because he knew it was his father's favorite kind of candy. ◯

8. "You are always picking on me! It isn't fair," Lisa snapped when her mother corrected her. ◯

9. Why can't you ever pack nice things in my lunch, like my friends have?" Benny whined at his mother. "I'm so tired of the same old stuff you give me." ◯

10. Barbara's mother told her to do all the dusting and set the table. Mother was outdoors, and would not see Barbara if she sat down and read her book for awhile! But Barbara decided to be obedient and finish all the work first. ◯

Do You Remember?

Here are some important words and names from this book. Can you match each one with the correct phrase on the right?

1. Edward Jenner
2. Plaque
3. Bacteria
4. Cardiac muscle
5. Louis Braille
6. Cochlea
7. Vertebrae
8. Calcium
9. Epiglottis
10. Vocal Cords
11. Stethoscope
12. Ultraviolet Rays
13. George Washington Carver
14. Cerebrum
15. Reflex
16. Alexander Graham Bell
17. Heredity
18. Posture
19. Water
20. Pituitary gland
21. Tolerance
22. Temperance
23. Shoplifting

a. fuzzy stuff that builds up on teeth
b. the muscles of your heart
c. fluid-filled tube in your ear
d. discovered how to prevent some diseases by vaccination
e. germs
f. made a special alphabet for the blind
g. your voice vibrators
h. a mineral in milk which helps build teeth and bones
i. your back bones
j. the lid on top your windpipe
k. the "thinking" part of your brain
l. a tool for listening to your heart
m. an automatic response by your body
n. rays of the sun that can be harmful
o. great Christian scientist
p. ways you are like your parents
q. courteously accepting others who are different
r. makes up two-thirds of your body weight.
s. sends out hormones which control growth
t. the way you hold your body
u. invented the telephone
v. stealing things in a store
w. self-control